People Who Have **Stolen** from Me

ALSO BY DAVID COHEN

Chasing the Red, White, and Blue

People Who Have **Stolen** from Me

David Cohen

PICADOR
ST. MARTIN'S PRESS
NEW YORK

www.picadorusa.com

Picador® is a U.S. registered trademark and is used by St. Martin's Press under license from Pan Books Limited.

For information on Picador Reading Group Guides, as well as ordering, please contact the Trade Marketing department at St. Martin's Press.
Phone: 1-800-221-7945 extension 763
Fax: 212-677-7456
E-mail: trademarketing@stmartins.com

Design by Nick Wunder

Library of Congress Cataloging-in-Publication Data Available upon Request

ISBN 0-312-42453-1
EAN 978-0312-42453-4

First published in the United States by St. Martin's Press

First Picador Edition: January 2005

10 9 8 7 6 5 4 3 2 1

For Pam

Contents

Some say South Africa's transition to democracy was a miracle. Given how many South Africans greeted democracy homeless, hungry, and jobless . . . it is indeed extraordinary that our formal institutions are stable, our polity reasonably settled. Could it be though that the rage so many expected found expression after all, not in the formal arenas of politics, but in the underworld of crime?

—JONNY STEINBERG, EDITOR OF *CRIME WAVE,*
WITWATERSRAND UNIVERSITY PRESS, 2001

If you fulfill the pattern that is peculiar to yourself—you have loved yourself, you have gained in abundance: You bestow virtue then because you have lustre, you radiate from your abundance, something overflows. But if you hate yourself, if you have not accepted your pattern, then there are hungry animals in your constitution which get at your neighbors like flies in order to satisfy the appetites which you have failed to satisfy. There is no radiation, no real warmth; there is hunger and secret stealing . . .

—ATTRIBUTED TO C. G. JUNG

Preface

The demise of apartheid and the birth of the new South Africa was one of the most celebrated and defining moments of the twentieth century. Decades of institutionalized racial discrimination and hundreds of years of oppression were finally ended in the last week of April 1994 when the country went to the polls and—in the first democratic elections in its history—voted in the African National Congress with Nelson Mandela as president. The world had high hopes for what could be achieved in the newly dubbed "rainbow nation" and promised to help by investing in the country and by vigorously reversing the economic, cultural, and political sanctions of the apartheid era.

During the apartheid years, and especially in the lead-up to the historic 1994 elections, South Africa was the focus of intense worldwide media scrutiny. Then, as so often happens after a cataclysmic event, it largely fell off the radar. The intimate portrait that fills these pages reveals a slice of what happened next.

The story takes place towards the end of the first decade of democratic rule and is set in a family business on Jules Street, a street officially recorded by the city elders as the longest straight street in Johannesburg—but on which crooked men thrive. Yes, nothing is quite as it seems. The book follows the tragicomic fortunes of two charismatic businessmen and their colorful coterie of employees—who include former carjackers—as they attempt to "get by" in the new South Africa.

For the white owners of the store who find themselves on the wrong end of a relentless crime wave, "getting by" means constantly shoring up their security and attempting to bring to justice the people—including their own trusted employees and, dramatically, even their own family members—who are stealing from them. Then there is the perspective of the stealers themselves—white, black, and Indian—who reveal their secret methods and motivations to the reader, but not always to their employers.

All at once, we are caught up in a myriad of vividly unfolding dramas that are reflective of personal, as well as national, dilemmas. For the furniture store is a thoroughfare through which almost the entire South African racial and social spectrum passes—white, black, Indian, mixed-race, middle class, and working class. And in this sense, it offers itself up as a fascinating microcosm of life—and morality—in South Africa today.

The broader context against which the narrative unfolds is that ten years into the new South Africa, crime has soared beyond all expectations to become the country's biggest growth industry. The official crime figures show that robbery has risen by an extraordinary 169 percent, housebreaking by 33 percent, cash heists, as well as carjacking, by 30 percent—and this off an already disturbingly high level of crime in 1994. To put this in global perspective, a recent survey of corporate crime by accountants PricewaterhouseCoopers shows that 71 percent of companies in South Africa report being the victims of fraud in the last two years, compared to 51 percent of businesses in the rest of Africa, and just 37 percent worldwide.

The repercussions of this crime wave are potentially catastrophic for the country as a whole and extend far beyond the immediate victims. For crime—and the fear it engenders—is the biggest cause of the brain drain and a critical deterrence to desperately needed foreign investment.

One could argue that it is, paradoxically, a measure of the extraordinary achievements of the new democratic South Africa that the country's main fault line is perhaps no longer between white and black, or communist and capitalist, or even rich and poor—but rather between the clean and the corrupt. Between those who opt to pursue their living by legitimate means, and those who, for whatever reason, choose the path of deception and crime. Between—to put it bluntly—the honest man and the crook. It may be that this division was always part and parcel of life in South Africa but was hitherto masked by the more obvious, deeper divisions wrought by apartheid. Perhaps. But something new and significant appears to be afoot here. And fresh solutions will be required to defeat it.

To a large extent, the crime wave is the unavoidable legacy of apartheid. It reflects the forced redistribution of wealth—the violent grab for economic power that has followed the much-heralded peaceful transfer of political power. For despite the expansion of the black middle class off the back of an aggressive black empowerment program, the country's wealth has remained largely in white hands. It will take more than a decade to right the wrongs of apartheid and to narrow the monumental gap between rich and poor. But—and this is the crunch—though ten years is but the blink of an eye in the life of a nation, it is a painfully long stretch in the lives of impatient young men who find themselves uneducated, unemployed, and without prospects. Just who has robbed whom? they want to know. And yet—difficult as this conundrum is to resolve—it is not the full story. Even harder to get to grips with is the evolution of the crime wave: why so many people involved in crime today are professionally organized, and in many cases, relatively well off. And why, for an increasing number of South Africans, theft has become a way of life.

It is this "way of life" that the book teases out. By reporting the dramatic events as they unfold in one particular store, I have attempted to show—rather than tell—how theft has woven itself into the daily fabric of social and business life, raising fundamental questions about trust between employers and employees, between family members, and between citizens. For without trust it is difficult—if not impossible—for a society to sustain itself.

In addition, the events portrayed raise serious questions that are not easy to answer. What bearing does historic injustice to an entire race of people have on present-day judgments as to who is innocent and who is guilty? How is one to behave as a moral person in a society in which law and order is severely compromised and immorality appears to have become the norm?

The reader should be aware that the story that follows is true, but that in most cases the names and identities of characters and businesses have been changed or disguised.

It is abundantly clear to me that I could not have written this book if I still lived in Johannesburg. (I grew up in Johannesburg, but since 1987 I have lived predominantly in London.) I would have been too close to the story, too immune to the extraordinary events unfolding on a daily basis, and I would not have had the broader perspective that the long lens brings. And yet, if I had *never* lived in South Africa, I may not have known my characters with the intimacy—as well as the sense of detachment—this book requires.

For to my eye, this is a story that goes beyond South Africa. The fundamental themes—of conscience, trust, and betrayal—that its characters grapple with are those that preoccupy ordinary people everywhere. They are universal. And the main characters—in their ability to endlessly and humorously entertain each other and in their resilient belief that things will eventually change for the better—are as timeless as Estragon and Vladimir in Samuel Beckett's *Waiting for Godot.*

People Who Have **Stolen** from Me

CHAPTER 1

Rearranging the Furniture

Six maxi-taxis fitted with crash bars cruise in single file towards their target. Each vehicle is manned by a driver and a helper and carries no passengers, only the essential tools: bolt cutters, hacksaws, blowtorches, and 9 mm revolvers. Their backseats are folded down and flattened in readiness. It is 2:35 A.M. There is no other traffic at this hour. The maxi-taxis purr down Jules Street, heading away from the Johannesburg city center, headlights casting low beams into the cool night air, and pull up at a forty-five-degree angle outside the lit-up premises of Jules Street Furnishers. The drivers cut their engines, kill their lights. They pull on their balaclavas, slide on their gloves. Then they grab the bolt cutters, hacksaws, and blowtorches and get to work.

Jules Street Furnishers is heavily fortified. The front elevation of the shop is comprised of a thick pane of reinforced shatterproof glass, especially toughened to withstand the force of hammers or bricks. The windows are further protected by two layers of burglar bars: solid steel bars fastened with state-of-the-art Abus locks are attached to the outside, and on the inside an expander security gate extends across the window from floor to ceiling like a concertina. The roof is protected by electrified barbed wire, and the entire premises is girded with alarms and wired to an armed response security firm whose operatives can be on site within three to five minutes of the alarm being triggered.

By 2:55 A.M., the men in balaclavas have blowtorched and cut the necks of the Abus locks. Working in pairs, they prize away the security grille to expose the naked pane of glass painted with grinning Easter bunnies and decorative lettering that promises EASTER SPECIALS!!!, even though Easter was months ago. There is the cough of an engine starting. The lead maxi-taxi backs up. The driver engages first gear, guns the engine, and accelerates towards the shop.

Piet van Staden is snoring into his Edblo king-size mattress in his flat across the road from Jules Street Furnishers when he is awakened by the almightiest crash he has ever heard. It is followed a second later by a siren venting its high-pitched fury into the night. He rushes to his balcony where he sees that a car has driven straight through the window of Jules Street Furnishers. He watches wide-eyed as the vehicle reverses and hooded figures run into the shop, emerging with TVs, hi-fis, and video recorders. He counts twelve men and six vehicles. They run in and out of the shop. In and out. In and out.

Ducking down so that he cannot be spotted, Piet reaches for his phone and dials the police.

The alarm, meanwhile, has activated the roving, gum-chewing operatives of the Instant Armed Response Security Company. At this hour, with the streets deserted, Hennie Hennops and his codriver know that they can be at Jules Street Furnishers within three minutes. But that risks a confrontation with the criminals and a gunfight. So Hennie does what he always does. He waits. Eight, ten minutes should do it. And then he drives like hell to "catch" them—hoping that they've gone.

By 3:02 A.M. the maxi-taxis are loaded up and, with a screeching of rubber, pull off into the night. The traffic lights on the corner blink red. A light rain starts to fall. Piet van Staden watches as the Instant Armed Response Security Company car roars up, followed in short order by the police.

Hennie Hennops strides through the gaping hole where the taxi has smashed through the window, his size-eleven boots crunching on the shattered glass underfoot, and surveys the scene. There are speakers lying on their sides, TV trolleys scattered about, sofas prostrate on their backs, twisted metal and glass everywhere. It is a scene of devastation. He pulls out his cell phone and calls the man he has listed as the owner of the shop.

The first thing Jack Rubin knows about any of this is when his wife, Julia, who is the lighter sleeper, elbows him sharply in the ribs. "Jack," he hears her saying as if from far away. "Jack, Jack, Jack, wake up, the phone is ringing."

"What time is it?" mumbles Jack, rolling out of bed. "Jeez! It's three in the morning." But he doesn't think, Who could this be? He feels a wave of nausea. He knows. There have been too many times before.

CHAPTER 2

Tea Time

On any given weekday 11 A.M. is tea time at Jules Street Furnishers. Tea time is also at 9 A.M., 1 P.M., 3 P.M., and 4 P.M.—selling furniture can be a thirsty business. At precisely two minutes before each of these appointed hours, Beauty Sithole climbs the steps from the showroom on the ground floor to the floor above. She walks slowly and deliberately past the carpet samples and the banks of Edblo mattresses sealed in plastic, past the stacks of Panasonic TVs, Kenwood hi-fis, Defy washing machines, and Electrolux vacuum cleaners. Beyond them, laid out in neat rows, are Draylon lounge suites—in floral greens and variegated blues, ruby reds and striped browns—all with prominently displayed pink price tags fastened securely with an elastic band. Beauty shuffles past the florid lounge suites and the rows of Formica-topped kitchen tables and the chipped, decorative porcelain swan, and she doesn't stop until she reaches the slamlock security gate to the office in the corner where Mr. Sher and Mr. Rubin have locked themselves in.

She stands there, bent metal tray in her hands, and rattles the security gate with her foot. From behind his desk, Harry Sher glances up from punching numbers into his Casio ticker tape adding machine. *Clack, clack, clack.* He is totaling up a pile of creditors' invoices, licking the end of his forefinger for traction as he riffles through the paperwork. Beauty waits patiently while he finishes the batch.

"Aaah, tea time," he says eventually. He walks down a transparent plastic runner laid over a well-worn carpet, unlocks the security gate, and is striding back across the runner when something occurs to him, and he spins round to face his business partner, Jack Rubin.

"I just don't get it, Rubin," he says.

"Pardon?" says Jack, looking up from the computer printout of debtors spread across his desk and dragging his cup of tea towards him.

"What's with these *tight* shirts of yours, Rubin?" Harry fluffs out his long, loose cufflinked sleeves and smoothes his tie, like a bird preening. "It's bad enough, Rubin, that you come to work without a jacket and tie. But do you have to wear those *tight* shirts." He pauses to dramatize his point, spitting out his *ts*. "Like *t-igh-t.*"

Jack leans back in his chair, an amused smile playing on his lips. "Seeing that the insults are starting to flow, Sher, just look at your color coordination. Tartan, green, and blue trousers. Can't you wear pants of just one color?"

"Nice, huh?" says Harry, deftly lifting a trouser leg to show off his sky-blue socks. "Blue mit da blue, green mit da green."

"Nice one, Sher. Blue shirt, green tie, blue socks, brown shoes, tartan, green-and-blue trousers. Very nice—if you're a peacock!"

"I don't expect you to know about such things, Rubin—you who dress like a throwback from the seventies—but according to the experts in these matters, as long as your socks match your shirt, you are sartorially correct."

"Well," counters Jack, "our definitions of sartorial correctness are obviously at variance."

"Nothing wrong," chuckles Harry, settling back into his chair, "nothing wrong."

He spreads the *Citizen* newspaper across his desk and skims it as he sips his tea. Jack returns to his work analysing unpaid debtors details, then picks up the phone to call Suzette Fish, one of their longest-serving managers.

"Okay, ask Suzette to phone me as soon as she's finished her meeting," he says. He grins broadly as he puts down the phone.

"Suzette's in a *meeting*," he repeats out loud. Harry chuckles without looking up. Suzette never has meetings. "Meeting" is their in-house code for "taking a crap."

Jack wants to ask Suzette whether Obi and Veli—their newest recruits—have come in to work yet. Suzette hired them on a freelance basis to tackle their most intractable cases of furniture repossessions in the townships. "They seem very firm in their manner, Mr. Rubin," Suzette had reported back. "I think they might be, like, quite good at debt collections and repos."

So Obi and Veli had been ushered upstairs where they sat on brown plastic chairs placed alongside each other on the plastic runner and where, briefly, Jack being out, Harry had interviewed them.

"What experience do you have in this business?" asked Harry.

"Sorry?" said Obi.

"What jobs did you do before?"

"Well, I can say that we were in business together," Obi replied.

"Oh?" said Harry, perking up. "And what kind of business was that?"

"The car business," said Obi.

"The car business," echoed Veli, his smoker's voice an octave deeper than Obi's.

"What kind of cars?"

Obi coughed sheepishly, shooting Veli a sideways glance. "Many cars."

"Many, many," repeated Veli.

"Our first job was a bakkie [pick-up truck], our second job was a Kombi, our third job was an Opel Kadette, our fourth was a Citi Golf, our . . ."

Harry looked momentarily nonplussed. "What you are telling me is . . ."

"Ya," said Obi, grinning self-consciously. "I want to be honest with you, Mr. Sher. We used to be hijackers."

Harry coughed.

"For three years," continued Obi. "Then I was arrested. I was eighteen months in jail."

"For me, too. I had the same problem," added Veli.

"And when you came out, did you stop?"

Obi nodded vigorously. "Yes, yes. We stopped." He paused. "But then, after a few months, we started again. I had made a certain girl pregnant. I had to support her."

"For me, too. I had the same problem," echoed Veli.

"But we are straight now, Mr. Sher." Obi smiled, flashing his gold-capped front tooth. "I look at it this way—we used to be in the car-repossession business, now we are in the furniture-repossession business."

Harry knew from bitter experience that good debt collectors were hard to find. Besides, he found himself drawn to their transparent candor and raffish charm. So he hired them. As to how recently they had given up their life of crime, he did not ask, and they did not tell.

They could hardly be more inept, or dishonest, he surmised, than their previous debt collectors. He had just fired the last lot, Plank and Marie Koekemoer, a little-and-large husband-and-wife team who could never walk through a door at the same time, and who had talked the game and looked the part but had turned out to be utterly useless. Before them Andries Barnard, with his potbelly, another one who had stolen from them, but that was another story. Besides, that *shmuck* had been hired by Rubin.

While Jack is waiting for Suzette to call so that he can instruct her to dispatch Obi and Veli on a job to repossess a lounge suite in Soweto, he takes a moment to test out their newly acquired swivel chair sitting unallocated in the corner. Jack had bought the chair from Fred van Staden, their insurance agent, who moved premises last week, and who had offered to sell them secondhand office equipment that had become surplus to his requirements. Jack gave Fred eight hundred rand [equivalent to approximately $100] and yesterday Fred had duly delivered a rickety, severely dented metal filing cabinet, a secondhand photocopier, and a swivel chair. The photocopier is a welcome replacement for their arthritic, ten-year-old machine that takes fifteen minutes to warm up and another five to deliver a single ink-smudged page. But the ergonomically designed swivel chair—*that* is the plum. And Harry and Jack have been coveting it greedily ever since it arrived.

"Why don't we spin for it?" suggests Harry warily, watching Jack rotating in the chair.

"Sure," says Jack, rising to his feet, slightly irritated. He is thinking that Harry should have the grace to let him have the chair. After all, who did the deal with van Staden? And eight hundred rand would have been a bargain just for the photocopier. But try and get a "well done" out of Sher! He pulls a two-rand coin from his pocket.

"Heads or tails, Sher?"

"Heads," says Harry. Jack sends the silver coin spinning through the air. Both men watch closely as the coin approaches the top of its arc and begins to drop back whereupon Jack catches it and slams it down onto his desk. He pulls his hand back and looks. "Tails," he declares, hastening over to claim his prize.

"Not so fast, Rubin, not so fast," says Harry, who strides over to inspect the coin for himself.

"That's heads."

"What do you mean that's heads?"

"The buck's head is heads," says Harry with a flourish. He flips over the coin. "There, the coat of arms, *that's* tails."

"Everyone knows the coat of arms is heads and the buck is tails," protests Jack. "The buck is heads," insists Harry. And before Jack can resist further, Harry has installed the new chair behind his desk and is leaning back on it, grinning triumphantly from ear to ear.

For almost four decades, Harry Sher and Jack Rubin have entertained each other with their ribald repartee and one-upmanship. They are not just business partners but brothers-in-law, too—Harry is married to Jack's older sister, Carmen. With their slicked-back silver-gray hair, dark glasses, and asymmetrical smiles, the two men look like a couple of Damon Runyon characters. At seventy-four, Harry is nine years older than Jack, but he prides himself on having the strength and fitness of a fifty-year-old. Sure, his nose is more spread around his face than he would like, but then Jack's appearance has its esoteric dimensions, too, his ears being unusually large and a little wayward. But both men are lean and healthy and have the kind of ruddy pallor that comes from living under the South African sun.

There, however, the similarities end. Personality-wise, the two men are polar opposites. Whereas Jack is even-tempered, Harry is hot-headed and excitable. Whereas Jack tends to remain unflustered under pressure, always trying to diplomatically defuse conflicts, Harry regards conflict as a win–lose situation that calls for intimidation and aggression. Whereas Jack is naturally understated, Harry is vividly animated. They approach life in totally different ways. Which is one of the reasons they make such excellent partners.

Although both Harry and Jack hold each other's attributes in high esteem, neither man is given to outward displays of affection, and they would never say as much. There are niggling tensions, too. Sometimes it irks Harry that Rubin doesn't give him the credit he feels he deserves. Would it have hurt Rubin to give him a "Well done!" when, through "brilliant sleuth work," he had discovered that it was Doubt Molefe, their shop steward, who was responsible for running up the exorbitant telephone bill of calls to a private cell phone on the company account? "But no, Rubin is as *tight* with his compliments as he is with his shirts."

And sometimes it frustrates Jack how Sher *always* has to be right. Few people on earth, he muses, are more competitive than Sher. The man can't even go for a jog with a friend without having to finish first. Even with his own children, now grown up, Sher was unable to hold back. Jack could remember watching Sher and his kids having long-jump competitions in the garden of their old home in the lower-middle-class suburb of Orange Grove. Sher would go hurtling through the air, beating Lauren, six, Jerry, four, and Lily, then just two years old, by several yards. "And once again," he would declare, "the winner is," . . . dramatic pause . . . "Harry Sher!" When the kids looked glum at having to assume the roles of perpetual losers, Harry would playfully admonish them, saying, "When you are good enough, you'll win, but until then, this is all about who comes *sssecond.*" Harry likes to grate his *tttttt*s and hiss his *sssss* to give his words maximum impact, and he embellishes his delivery with grand hand movements. Sometimes Harry would tell his children, "Your father is the richest man in Orange Grove." Whether this was true or not was beside the point. Nobody knew better than they, and Jack, that Sher had an insatiable need to be a winner.

"Okay Sher, you can have the chair," surrenders Jack. "I'm quite happy with mine anyway." Jack has convinced himself that he doesn't really want the new swivel chair. Frankly, it isn't as comfortable as it looks. He laughs. Let Sher enjoy his win.

But Harry isn't finished. "Have you ever noticed," he says, flashing a self-satisfied grin, "that there is a difference in laugh between a winner and a loser? Have you ever noticed that they *laugh* differently? The winner . . . well, I wouldn't say it's a gloating laugh, let's call it a victorious laugh. The loser? It's always a philosophic laugh, it's always *only a chair!*"

The phone rings. "That'll be Suzette," notes Jack. "She must be finished her m-e-e-ting." But it isn't Suzette. It's their stock controller, Misty Naidoo, calling from their downtown branch, where Harry's younger brother, Ronny Sher, is the manager.

"Mr. Rubin, something has happened," she says, swallowing her words in panic.

"What is it?" says Jack.

"According to my stock book, there is a whole lot of stock that is supposed to be here, but I can't find it in the shop."

The color drains from Jack's face. "How much?"

"More than fifty thousand rand, Mr. Rubin."

"What are you talking about, Misty? How can fifty thousand rand's worth of stock suddenly go missing?" Misty is silent, breathing heavily. "Misty," says Jack, speaking slowly and deliberately, "I want you to go over the books with a fine-tooth comb with Ronny Sher and detail exactly—exactly—what is missing. I want you to call me back as soon as you're done."

Jack replaces the receiver and—after conferring with Harry—calls Jamal Suliman, who, until they had promoted him to manager of their Germiston branch last month, had been Ronny Sher's assistant manager in their downtown branch. "Misty has discovered that stock is missing," he tells Jamal tersely. "You better go downtown and sort out what's going on with Ronny."

Twenty minutes later, Jack's phone rings. This time it's Ronny. "Things are not looking good," he tells Jack. "I think you better come over."

CHAPTER 3

The Longest Straight Street in Johannesburg

Jules Street runs without a kink, straight as a ruler, from the edge of downtown Johannesburg, and heads inexorably east to the very rim of the city limit. Its history is largely undocumented, its place in the pantheon of streets unrecognized, but at precisely 5.8 kilometers long, Jules Street has a unique claim to fame: It was once recorded by the city's elders as the longest straight street in Johannesburg.

"I wish to inform you that Jules Street is officially now the longest straight road in Johannesburg," the town clerk told editors at the *Star* newspaper on August 1, 1958. Presumably it was a slow news day, but this little tidbit of trivia made the papers, and thereafter the reputation of Jules Street was assured. Over the following decades, this extraordinary feature of an otherwise ordinary street has been stretched to its limit, so that Jules Street—pronounced "Jewels Street"—is unblinkingly referred to by many of its residents as the longest straight street in South Africa. Sometimes, in moments of unbridled enthusiasm, all qualifying adjectives are dropped and it is simply claimed that Jules Street is the longest straight street in Africa.

Harry and Jack know all about this, being both denizens of the street and inveterate collectors of trivia. But what they also know through personal experience is that, on this longest straight street almost everyone is crooked.

The fact is that they run their business in the face of what, in a normal society, would be regarded as impossible odds. Professional gangs of criminals ram-raid their shop and cart off their merchandise in the dead of night. Armed robbers walk in off the street and hold them up on a regular basis.

Presently, one in five of their customers is failing to fulfill payment obligations, resulting in bad debts approaching an extraordinary 20 percent of turnover. But worst of all is the secret stealing from within, by some of their own trusted managers, whom they discover are robbing them blind.

Both men welcome the democracy that defines the new South Africa, in every way an improvement on the old, they say, except one: crime. In the last ten years, and especially the last five, their shop, their block, their street, has been in the grip of a crime wave that is as brutal as it is unrelenting.

It is not that Jules Street has been earmarked for special treatment. Violent crime is out of control throughout the city and the broader Johannesburg region and blacks are as likely to be victims as whites. In some ways, this makes the assaults harder to cope with, because one can feel there is no escape. But it also makes life easier to bear, because you surrender to the big flow, to something that is larger than just you and your street. You are in it together. What makes the crime wave so frightening, though, is that it is so random. No one—neither the wealthy nor the poor— is immune.

From a practical point of view, people respond in different ways. "You modify your behavior to feel safe," Harry explains. Since Harry was carjacked outside his house by two men brandishing AK-47s not long ago, he takes a different route to and from work each day to make sure he is not being followed. "You make adjustments to the way you live, but, after that, you can't let it get to you," he says. Some people, though, feel a need to directly address the crime and the anxiety it brings—constantly broaching the subject at dinner tables, or seeking the counsel of trauma counselors. Still others prefer, as does Jack's wife, Julia, to carry on with life regardless, and not to alter their behavior, or to discuss it at all. Often, the extent to which people need to talk is a factor of how recently they, or a friend, or a member of their family, have been a direct victim. Sometimes, especially among the middle-class whites that Harry and Jack mix with, the conversation is shot through with denial, especially when they find themselves in the presence of friends or relatives who use the crime problem to justify a decision to emigrate. It's then that they privately put the crime into personal perspective: as a price they are reluctantly prepared to pay for the high standards of living they enjoy, and would struggle to replicate elsewhere. For, despite its problems, Jules Street Furnishers has sustained two families for four decades, sending seven children—Harry's three and Jack's four—to university. And it has never had a year when it has not been profitable.

But there is something more. When you are staying put in South Africa—as Harry and Jack are—you have to develop ways of living in it. "We love our country," says Jack. "We are not leaving. When you take that position, you *have* to be optimistic. It doesn't mean we put our heads in the sand. Far from it. We deal with the daily reality. What it does mean is that in between the crime, which, as I say, we have to deal with, we become attuned to looking for green shoots of progress. We remind ourselves that our constitution is one of the finest in the world, that we've had a peaceful transition to democracy, that it's only a new democracy, and that all democracies take time to settle. We have all these black kids coming through the schools and going to universities now, a rising black middle class, and generally the feeling between the races—in our shops and in the suburbs—is a good one. There is no animosity. These positive signs feed our optimism and sustain us."

In truth, Jules Street Furnishers is a rather unglamorous middle-of-the-road chain of furniture stores, and does not present itself as an especially tantalizing target for criminals. It comprises an archipelago of six branches scattered around the city, each one selling mainly on credit—or what is locally termed "hire purchase"—to a working-class customer base.

They sell on hire purchase not out of choice, but because that is the traditional business model for retailing furniture to the working classes, both black and white, in South Africa. Unlike America and other developed western nations, where few furniture chains still extend credit to individual customers but are happy to take payment by credit card, thereby transferring all risk of nonpayment to the credit card companies, South Africa is a less sophisticated market. A significant proportion of the population does not even possess bank accounts, let alone credit cards, and, for this reason, businesses like Jules Street Furnishers have no alternative but to sell on credit to customers who typically spread repayment of their debt over a two-year period.

Their largest and flagship branch—which doubles as their head office—is situated towards the eastern end of Jules Street. From here, on the second floor, in an office not much larger than a boxing ring, Harry and Jack direct their empire. Once there were eleven furniture shops situated along the length of Jules Street, but now there are only three. The others have gone out of business or moved away, unable to adjust to the new South Africa and the demographic changes it wrought.

In the sixties and seventies and up until the early eighties Jules Street was a sedate, white, blue-collar street with a mix of residential, retail, and commercial properties. Black people and Asians were barred from living or owning businesses there. By the mideighties, however, as apartheid began to fray at the edges, blacks moved in from surrounding townships, creating gray areas in contravention of the soon-to-be-defunct Group Areas Act. In a few short years, central Johannesburg—otherwise known as "downtown"—was released to take on its destiny, that of a vibrant, anarchic African city. Even before the new South Africa officially arrived in 1994, Jules Street had become a rambunctious street typical of Africa, replete with unlicensed street vendors, illegal drinking establishments known as shebeens, cacophonic sports bars, and colorful street barbers.

The accompanying demographic shift fundamentally altered the nature of business on Jules Street. Harry and Jack's customer base swung dramatically from 80 percent working-class white to 90 percent black. But, whereas many of their fellow white businessmen fled north over the Parktown ridge to the wealthy white suburbs beyond, relocating their businesses, Harry and Jack stayed put. Rather than sell out or shut up shop—or perhaps simply unable to do so—they attempted to adjust, just as they had to the earlier demographic shift when the Portuguese moved into Jules Street back in the seventies.

The African character of the street is apparent from the scene directly outside the front door of Jules Street Furnishers. Black female hawkers sit barefoot and cross-legged on the hot pavement in the blazing midday sun and peddle fruit and vegetables. Their stock is arranged in meager pyramids and comprises tomatoes, onions, apples, and mangos, just two rand [$0.25] for eight pieces. They also sell handfuls of nuts, chocolate eclair sweets in wrappers, and Chappie chewing gum, for one rand.

On the corner, beyond the hooting and shouting of the chaotic pull-in, pull-out taxi rank, smoke drifts up from mobile kitchens and the enticing aroma of open-air cooking is carried on the breeze. At one end of the block a young woman by the name of Princess Nzo prepares pots of steaming hot curried *pap en vleis* (maize meal and meat) which she sells for ten rand a plate. She does a brisk trade with the factory workers who work to the south of the street, a few hundred yards away down towards the railway line. On the other corner a young man, Sipho Mfolo, caters to the bottom end of the street food market. He barbecues cow's intestines and hearts, charging three rand for an intestine, seven rand for a heart. It's an acquired taste for which there is significantly less demand. Bloody, uncooked portions are protected by a flimsy piece of plastic wrap in a vain attempt to ward off the growing horde of flies that congregate in the midday sun.

A few doors down from Jules Street Furnishers, a doctor's surgery is open for business. Here, a single doctor is assisted by a bored receptionist who sits feet up on an adjacent chair, head buried in a women's magazine. Her job is to collect weapons from the patients who attend the walk-in surgery. As the sign behind her desk makes clear: "Under no circumstances will any firearms or sharp objects (knives) be allowed in the doctor's rooms. Kindly leave these items with the receptionist."

Directly alongside Jules Street Furnishers, a down-market sports café opens onto the street, offering customers a darkened room with a bare concrete floor, a pool table, a service counter, a TV and a hi-fi. Heavy rock and garage music blares—*doef, doef, doef*—all day and much of the night from their partially-blown speakers. Unemployed young men—among them illegal immigrants from Nigeria and Mozambique—lounge about and shoot pool, their eyes disturbingly bloodshot as they drink cardboard cartons of Joburg Beer, a cheap lager that advertises itself as "the taste of the big city."

It is not a place that Harry or Jack—or their employees for that matter—would ever frequent. Nor does its presence do anything to lure respectable customers to their end of the street. But after a while, say Harry and Jack, you simply grow used to the discordant noise and stop noticing it. Like the vendors and taxi drivers, informal drinking houses like these have sprung up all along the street and have become an integral part of the Jules Street scene.

CHAPTER 4

Driving Jules Street

This morning like all mornings, Jack's car, a ten-year-old white Mercedes, is parked outside the shop. It is being watched over by Cain Radebe, their security guard, who stands on a tree stump, armed only with a truncheon, lost in thought. Like a human scarecrow, Cain's presence is meant to deter would-be thieves, but in practice there isn't much he can do. Just three weeks ago four armed men walked into Jules Street Furnishers and cleaned them out of cell phones worth twelve thousand rand. As the robbers were making their getaway, one of the saleswomen alerted Cain, who had been dozing on the stump, and who sprang impressively into action, sprinting after them in hot pursuit. Cain was gaining ground on the laden robbers as they raced down Jules Street, dodging between fruit vendors and watch vendors and sneaker vendors and leapfrogging traffic, when suddenly one of the robbers stopped in his tracks, spun round, and put a gun to Cain's head.

"Do you want to die for your white bosses?" he barked at him.

"Turn around and go back to the shop. They are insured. They can afford it."

So Cain promptly turned tail and came trotting back to the shop. He reported his conversation with the robbers to Mr. Sher and Mr. Rubin. Then he resumed his position on the stump.

In order to get from the head office to the downtown branch of Jules Street Furnishers, Jack must drive west towards town, taking in almost the entire length of Jules Street. From here, although they are almost six kilometers away, the straightness of the street affords Jack an unimpeded view of the skyscrapers of the Johannesburg city center. To the south of the street, to his left as he drives, are factories and a railway line, and just beyond them are the golden mine dumps that mark the spot of some of the most famous mines in South Africa: Simmer & Jack, Primrose, City Deep. The richest gold reef in the world broke ground a few hundred yards south of Jules Street and originally, at the turn of the twentieth century, Jules Street evolved as the residential and retail hub for the hard-hatted white and black miners who worked this part of the reef. But today most of these gold mines are mined out, and mining has receded from the consciousness of the people who live and work here.

Jules Street unfurls like a black ribbon through three suburbs—Malvern at its eastern extremity, Belgravia in the middle, and Jeppe at the town end—and the character of the street changes markedly as you travel from one side to the other.

The Malvern end, where Jules Street Furnishers is located, is the most vibrant and commercially viable part of the street. It is along this portion that most of the retailers, banks, butchers, sports cafes, nightclubs, liquor stores, fast-food restaurants, supermarkets, pawn shops, street vendors, and taxi ranks are situated, usually with residential accommodation attached to the back of the shops, and on top as well, to the second- and third-floor levels. Here, Jules Street is a hodgepodge of architectural styles—row houses interspersed with semi-detached houses, as well as the old-fashioned house-attached-to-the-shop design—reflecting its mixed residential and commercial zoning and lack of coherent town planning. But the street itself is confident and broad, four lanes wide, two in each direction, with an extra lane on each side for parked vehicles.

The middle segment of the street, the Belgravia section, is dominated by the infamous car dealerships that have made Jules Street the secondhand car mecca of Johannesburg. They sit cheek by jowl, dozens and dozens of them, painted in gaudy pinks, luminous tangerines, and bright purples, separated only by motor accessory shops and innumerable car washes. "Best cheapies in town," "Cars wanted for cash," declare the garish billboards above lots and pavements crammed with secondhand cars parked tightly in rows. Further on are the dilapidated, once grand hotels of Belgravia—such as the Casino Hotel, with its red tin roof, brown pillars, and beige awnings—faded reminders of the days, one hundred years ago, when Belgravia was an address to be proud of. After a few kilometers the dealerships peter out into grim, low-slung hostels housing black manual workers, and further on, some low-grade public housing for poor, mainly elderly, whites.

The western end of Jules Street is the most forlorn. It edges its way, just a single lane in each direction, into the forgotten southeastern corner of town. Here the oil-stained street has an industrial flavor and is lined on both sides by vandalized warehouses, small engineering and electrical workshops, and grimy car repair shops. An abandoned, rusting silver Mercedes, with a bullet hole through the windscreen blocks the pavement. There are few pedestrians anyway. Jules Street ends—or some would say begins—at a derelict industrial building of brick and glass, boarded up and abandoned, with its windows smashed to smithereens. From here the road continues for a few hundred yards, but no longer as Jules Street. This, the roadside paving stone informs you, is now Durban Street.

As Jack drives he has one ear to the radio. The program host, Tim Modise, is talking to the author of a new book on AIDS. "It is said that 10 percent of the population, 4.2 million South Africans, are HIV-positive," Modise is saying. More than fifteen hundred South Africans are infected with HIV every day, and almost the same number are dying on a daily basis. The average life expectancy in the country is plummeting from sixty-eight years to an estimated, pitiful thirty-six years by the year 2010. It is a time bomb, he continues, that is predicted to have devastating social and economic consequences for the growth of the country.

On Jack's passenger seat, under a pile of mail, is the death certificate of one of their security guards, Isaac Zuma, just thirty-one years old. "Two months ago Isaac got sick," says Jack grimly. "He had only been with us a few months when he said that he had to go back up north to be with his wife. We didn't know what the story was. But when I got this certificate—saying that he died of 'pneumonia'—I knew."

AIDS is a problem, notes Jack, that reaches into the heart of every business, especially businesses that cater to the poorer sections of the population, like Jules Street Furnishers. "If AIDS is 10 percent in the population, then you can take it as read that at least 10 percent of our customers—and staff—have it," says Jack. "The terrible thing about AIDS is that it kills our people at an age when they are economically most active. It's not like one of those old person's diseases, like cancer; this one fucks you up in your twenties and thirties, when you're a young father or mother.

"And who is there to look after their families when they're gone? We have to think about that, because, to put it plainly, at the end of the day we have a business to run. Who will pay their debts? One month, they are coming in regularly to pay their account, the next they have disappeared, gone back to their homeland to die among their extended families. For them and their families it's a tragedy. But it's hard for us, too, because we are left to pick up the pieces. In our case, we are left with a large bad debt that has to be written off."

The soaring level of bad debts—a whopping 19 percent of their turnover—has been on Jack's mind lately. "There is an old saying in the furniture business," he muses, "that if you have too few bad debts, you are being too conservative in your credit policy, and that if you have too many, you are being too lax. The secret of this business is to give credit to good risks—people in stable employment, with a history of residence and decent references. We will have to tighten our system because our bad debts are running at twice the industry acceptable level."

There have been times when Jack and Harry have become so exasperated with chasing down recalcitrant debtors that they have considered selling out and going into an entirely different kind of business altogether. "Once, we actually went so far as to call in a business broker," admits Jack. "We sat him down and he said to us: 'Okay, what kind of business are you looking for?'

" 'We want a good *cash* business,' we told him. 'What kind of a cash business?' he pressed us. 'Any kind, we don't care, as long as it's a good cash business.' 'Is that so?' he says to us. 'Is that so? Well, I'll tell you what I've got.' He rummaged through his papers. 'It just so happens that I've got an incredible cash business that the owner wants to sell right now. An incredible one.' 'Yes?' we said. 'It's the fish and chips shop at Johannesburg railway station.' 'A fish and chips shop?' Harry and I threw up our hands in horror. 'This guy wants to sell his business,' the broker explained, 'because, when he goes to bed at night, however many times he washes himself, he can't get rid of the smell of fish and chips!' "

Jack gives a broad grin. "So, after that we decided to stay in our own business. You realize that all businesses have problems, even cash ones. As a friend of mine likes to say: 'Why is the grass greener on the other side? Because there's more shit.'"

As Jack cruises down Jules Street, trying to coordinate his speed with the timing of the traffic lights, he reflects on how violent crime has eliminated certain businesses from the street. Jules Street was once home to some of the best Portuguese restaurants in the city, but every one of them are now gone. Campino's, perhaps the best-known of these establishments, closed down a few years ago when the owner was brutally murdered—apparently for the daily takings. The owner of Mustang Sally's Café Restaurant was killed too, says Jack, as was the owner of Pop's Supermarket, who, rumor has it, was shot at point-blank range in front of the shoppers.

The crime wave has also caused two banks to close their doors and leave the street. The remaining banks—including First National Bank, where Jules Street Furnishers have their account—have spent millions of rands upgrading their security. Anyone who enters the Jules Street branch of First National Bank is first frisked by a uniformed security guard with a handheld metal detector. Then they pass into a sealed, bulletproof glass booth where they are x-rayed by a second automated metal detector. "Metal has been detected," a disembodied mechanical voice booms back at you. "Place all firearms and all objects on the shelf and step back to be recleared."

Stringent measures like these have become standard in almost all branches of all banks in Johannesburg—not just on Jules Street—and with them, the banks believed they had gone a long way to foiling the bank robbers. But, canny as the banks have become, so too have the criminals. The latest ruse, recounts Jack, was by a woman in a wheelchair who asked to be allowed in through the side door because her wheelchair couldn't fit through the booth with the metal detector. As soon as she was inside, she lifted the blanket covering her legs to reveal three guns and a couple of hand grenades. Suddenly her legs worked fine, and together with her accomplices, who were waiting inside, they held up the bank and got away with undisclosed hundreds of thousands of rands.

Violent crime has become an everyday reality in Johannesburg, says Jack, and its citizens have developed strategies to cope with it. Jack's response is a practical one: He goes to the bank as seldom as possible. He adopted this strategy after the day he himself was attacked. Jack never tells anyone this story, not even his children. He doesn't want to alarm them, he says, least of all his youngest daughter, who lives with her husband and young children in Johannesburg. (Jack's son and two older daughters live in London and New York, respectively.) "It's over. I survived. Why dwell?" he says.

It happened one morning about seven or eight years ago, when Jack drove to First National Bank on Jules Street to deposit the previous day's cash takings, which he carried with him in an old leather briefcase. On this morning, having made his deposit, Jack left the bank with an empty briefcase and drove—just as he is doing today—to the downtown branch. Then, as now, Jack turned right out of Jules Street, swung left into Anderson, and soon pulled up across the road from their downtown branch. In those days, says Jack, he didn't even bother to lock his car doors.

But this time he had been followed.

"As I switch off the engine," recalls Jack, "the passenger door is wrenched open and I see this man with a knife, half concealed inside a newspaper, reach for the briefcase on the seat. Before he can get it, I grab the briefcase, yank open my door, jump out, and scream: "Fuck off!" He slams the passenger door shut and for a split second, we face each other, eye to eye, across the body of the car. I notice that he is lean and agile, in his twenties, and not nervous at all, despite the fact that it is broad daylight and there are other people in the street. And then I'm running. I'm fifty-seven years old, and yet I'm surging like the hundred-meter sprinter I used to be back in high school.

"But then out of the corner of my eye I see a second guy coming towards me, also with a knife in a newspaper. So I check my run and change direction. I run back around the front of the car to get away from the second guy, but now the first guy is closing in on me. It flashes through my head that the briefcase is empty. What am I protecting? Let him have the *chazzisher* case. So, at three yards, I throw the briefcase at the guy, and he catches it. I dart across the road and into our shop. As I get inside I see the two criminals jump into a green BMW with my empty briefcase. They roar off, almost crashing into a police car coming the other way, and then they're gone. Meanwhile, my heart is beating wildly. The staff sit me down, bring me a glass of water.

"'Mr. Rubin, your shirt!' one of the sales ladies cries. 'Mr.

Rubin, there's blood all over it!' I roll up my sleeve and I see that my arm is cut next to the artery. He must have nicked me when I grabbed the briefcase, but my adrenaline was pumping so hard I didn't even feel it."

Soon after that, Harry and Jack hired a firm of security guards to do their banking for them.

But this memory is suddenly far from Jack's mind as he parks his Mercedes and enters their downtown branch, a rambling store situated in an apricot-colored building with original Cape-Dutch architecture, and where twenty-four hi-fis are blaring at once.

Instead, some niggling, unpleasant questions are elbowing their way to the forefront of his consciousness. How can so much stock go missing and Ronny know nothing about it? Is Harry's brother involved in this?

CHAPTER 5

Secret Stealing

J amal Suliman had done his best to tactfully turn down his promotion. "Thank you, thank you, I am pleased you think so highly of me," he had told Mr. Rubin with a slight inclination of his head, "but really I would prefer to stay in the downtown shop where I am happy."

Harry and Jack, who wanted to promote Jamal from assistant manager of their downtown shop to the newly vacated manager position of their Germiston branch, had been taken aback, not least because the promotion meant more money for Jamal. "Why don't you want to move?" they asked him.

Jamal had to think fast, but what he told them was essentially true. "As you know, I recently bought a ten-seater VW Kombi van," he said, "and in order to pay it off I run a kind of a taxi service, ferrying people between Lenasia and town every morning and evening. If I moved to Germiston, it would make it difficult to operate, because I would be, like, quite far from town, you know."

But Harry and Jack didn't know, and they didn't want to know.

They weren't employing Jamal to run his own private taxi service. They insisted that Jamal go where he was needed and accept the promotion.

There was another reason Jamal didn't want to move, though this he dared not share with Mr. Sher or Mr. Rubin. Instead, he talked over his misgivings with Ronny Sher, Harry's younger brother and his manager, whom he regarded as his friend.

"Don't worry," Ronny breezily reassured him. "Nothing will go wrong. Nobody will find out."

But now, as Jamal drives to the downtown branch, the situation he feared most has come about. He doesn't want to do anything silly, but he is so nervous he can hardly hold the steering wheel. He is a frail man and has no stomach for this, and his first instinct is to come clean, to just confess, to throw himself at their mercy. He feels nauseated at the thought of what will happen to him, now that it will all come out. Mr. Rubin and Mr. Sher are decent sorts, he reassures himself. They will shout at first, especially Mr. Sher—boy, can he get *woes*—but then they will offer him another chance.

They know he comes from a decent, law-abiding Moslem family, he reasons. They know his brother-in-law, whom they have long employed as a manager in another branch, and they will take this into account as well. He has no criminal record. In fact, his friends regard him as somewhat of a model: a family man, forty-four years old, faithfully married for twenty-one years to Sanji, with three children, and house-proud to boot, living in an immaculate rental home in Lenasia South.

His thoughts turn to Sanji, who knows nothing of all this. How will he explain?

Jamal pulls up and parks his VW Kombi behind Mr. Rubin's white Mercedes outside the downtown branch. Inside, he sees Ronny officiously directing operations, sending piles of ledgers and stock books over to Mr. Rubin in the far corner. At first, Ronny appears to ignore Jamal, giving him a frosty reception. He has seen Ronny get like this sometimes. But when nobody is looking, Ronny pulls Jamal to one side and whispers in a low, intense tone. "I had to tell them what you did," he says. "Look Jamal, if you keep me out of it, I promise I'll help you pay it back. The worst that can happen is that you will have to pay them back. Keep your head. I'll put in a good word. I'm sure they'll let you keep your job."

An hour later, Jamal is on his way to the head office on Jules Street. He sits in the passenger seat alongside Mr. Rubin, ashen-faced, silent, trying to hold back the tears.

Jack ushers Jamal through the slamlock security gate into the office where Harry Sher is waiting. Jamal walks gingerly down the plastic runner and perches on the brown plastic chair that has been pulled out, awaiting his arrival.

"Stock is missing," Jack begins plainly. "What do you know about it, Jamal?"

Jamal's hands are shaking. He takes a deep breath. "Yes," he nods. "I do know what happened."

"Well?"

"That stock that is missing is not really missing, Mr. Rubin."

"What are you talking about?"

"I mean—it was sold for cash."

"Where is the money then?"

"I want to ask your forgiveness, Mr. Rubin. It was me who took the money."

Harry has been forbiddingly silent, but now he stands, red in the face, unable to restrain his anger. "You're a fucking crook, Jamal," he shouts. "We trusted you. We gave you a chance. We even gave you a promotion. This is how you repay us!"

Jamal has never seen Mr. Sher so upset.

"I will pay back every cent," says Jamal. "I promise to pay back every cent."

"How will you do that, Jamal?" says Jack. "There is more than fifty thousand rand missing. Where will you get the money?"

"Ronny will help me. Ronny says he will help me pay it back."

Harry takes a deep breath. He walks back around his desk, straightens his tie, composes himself. "Why would Ronny help you, Jamal? Why would Ronny help you? Does Ronny know anything about this?"

Jamal's head is pounding. He wants to make a clean breast of it. He avoids Mr. Sher's eyes bearing down on him like pistons. He anxiously scratches his beard. The urge to come clean is overwhelming. But at the same time he needs to be strategic. His association with Mr. Sher and Mr. Rubin, as he always refers to them, has been a long one, and he hopes it can continue.

Jamal first met Mr. Sher and Mr. Rubin back in 1980 when he became a customer of Jules Street Furnishers. Newly married, he and Sanji had moved into unfurnished rental rooms, and for the first time in his life he was buying furniture. He bought a bedroom suite, a kitchen unit, a stove, a kettle, and an iron. The bed was a standard double with a headboard, and it included a dressing table with an oak finish. He remembered the bed, because it was the most expensive thing he had ever bought, and because his children were conceived on it. The whole lot came to eight hundred rand and he opened an account, the plan being that he would pay it off in monthly installments over two years.

In the ensuing years Jamal bought more furniture from Jules Street Furnishers. Then, one Saturday morning he came into the shop to pay his regular installment and fell into a conversation with Mr. Rubin. "There was something in him that made me feel I could talk to him," Jamal recalls. "He had a very approachable manner. He seemed a kind person. I told Mr. Rubin that I was working for an electrical company that was relocating to Pretoria and I was worried about such a long commute. I hinted that I was looking to improve my job prospects. He said he would keep me in mind, that maybe they had something."

About three weeks later, recalls Jamal, Mr. Rubin phoned and asked him to come in. "He offered me a job as a salesman at the downtown branch. He started me at seven hundred and fifty rand a month, a fifty-rand increase over my previous job."

"I still remember my first day of work. It was May 5, 1984. I walked into the downtown branch, and that was the first time I met Ronny Sher. He was the manager and he was expecting me. He asked me if I knew anything about selling furniture.

"I said, 'No, this is my first time.'

"'Okay,' he said. 'I'll teach you. You need to know how to approach customers, how to have the right posture, how to talk to them.'

"Ronny treated me well. In the beginning he was hard on me. I suppose he had to be to teach me. He would quite often shout at me, embarrass me in front of customers. 'That's not the way to talk to customers! That's not the way to stand!' he would say. But in truth, I did not know how to sell, and Ronny taught me everything he knew. There were eight of us in the shop. Ronny was the only white. I was the only Indian. The rest of the staff were black.

"Ronny had sales targets that the shop had to meet in order for us to get our bonuses, and in order to meet those targets we had to sell. Ronny himself had a unique manner with customers who, in the downtown shop, were mainly black factory workers. He would address each customer the same. 'Come here, customer,' he would say. 'What would you like to buy, customer?' He never addressed them by their name. That was his way of putting himself above them. Because he was white."

Ronny always presented himself as the reasonable man. Mr. Average. Mr. Dependable. Mr. Model Citizen. He was the secretary of his tennis club, a committee man, a civic man, and a family man. Jamal valued these qualities, not least because he aspired to them himself.

Ronny was also a man of meticulous habit. He would open the shop at 8 A.M. every morning, and then at 8:15 A.M. he would disappear into the toilet with his newspaper, emerging ten minutes later, so that by 8:25 A.M. he'd be back at his desk. This was the signal for one of the black sales ladies to deliver him his first cup of tea and his jam donut, bought with till money from the bakery on the corner. By 8:30 A.M. he had consumed his tea, devoured his jam donut, wiped the crumbs off his distinctive handlebar mustache, and was ready to tackle the day.

"Hello, customer!" he would beam expansively.

One of Jamal's jobs was to spin discs—long-playing records—

on the hi-fi, featuring hit-parade bands and solo artists from popular black music labels such as *Smanje Manje,* in order to entice passing black customers into the shop. After two years of selling and spinning, Jamal was promoted to assistant manager.

"After a while Ronny and I began to develop a real relationship," he says. "We'd eat together at lunch time, he with his sandwiches made by his wife, and me with my sandwiches made by my wife. If I bought a Coke, I'd buy him one, too, and he'd do the same for me. We had a lot of laughs. In fact, I can say that Ronny was my first white friend. He invited me to his son's bar mitzvah. And twice he invited my wife and me to his house for dinner. It was the 1980s. Not many whites did that. I trusted Ronny—in the beginning."

Initially, Jamal never had much to do with Mr. Sher, because Mr. Rubin was in charge of the branches, but the little contact he did have was instructive. "I learned that Mr. Sher was a very straightforward person. I could say blunt. He would tell you straight to your face if something was wrong. Straight. You can see right away in his face if he is in a good mood or a bad mood. He could shit you out in front of staff or customers. He could use vulgar words. But he could also be kind and generous. When I needed money to buy my first car he helped me. He took Ronny aside. 'Just give Jamal the two thousand rand he needs. Deduct one hundred rand a month from his salary,' he told him. They were prepared to bend, to help. Mr. Rubin was different. He never used vulgar words. If I upset him he would call me aside. He would never say anything in front of other people. We were close, me and Mr. Rubin. Anything I need, I could speak freely to Mr. Rubin."

Jamal noticed that Mr. Sher seemed to keep his harshest words for his brother Ronny. "He would treat Ronny as a worker, as a member of staff, not a brother. He would often arrive and start shouting at Ronny because something wasn't right in the shop. Sometimes Ronny spoke rudely to the staff in front of customers, and the staff would complain to Mr. Sher. Mr. Sher would just take off at Ronny. 'Don't talk to the staff that way! Don't bladdy tell me your *bobbeh-meissehs!*' The problem was that he did it to Ronny in front of all of us. 'I'm sorry,' Ronny would say. 'It won't happen again.' Ronny became very quiet."

"Harry," Ronny later told Jamal, "is not the sort of person you want to cross."

"I think Ronny was scared of his brother. But he respected him, too. The odd thing was that he was more scared of Mr. Rubin. Even more. Frightened and resentful. At the time, I didn't know why. When I was still new there, I think Mr. Rubin had caught him doing something he shouldn't have been doing. There was a lot of tension for a while between Ronny on one hand, and Mr. Sher and Mr. Rubin on the other. Ronny never told me why, and I didn't ask. After about six months the tension subsided, but still Ronny remained wary of his brother, and especially of Mr. Rubin. Mr. Rubin was the same age as Ronny. I think he resented that Mr. Rubin was his brother's partner. Maybe he thought he should have been a partner, too. Mr. Rubin used to come around twice a week to check on Ronny. I can tell you, Ronny was happy when he left the shop."

As time went by Jamal began to realize that Ronny was not an entirely honest person. "He was running lots of little schemes. One involved TV licenses. He used to take the customer's money for TV licenses, but instead of going to the post office and taking out the license for the customer, he put the money in his pocket. He said it wasn't really stealing, because he was only taking from the post office."

One day Jamal and Ronny each got a phone call asking them to come to Mr. Sher's house that evening and to bring their wives. When Jamal arrived with Sanji, Mr. Rubin was there, and Ronny and his wife, Louise, were already seated on the sofa.

"Do you know why we've called you here?" Mr. Sher had begun.

"No," said Ronny.

"I've got no idea," concurred Jamal.

Mr. Sher then leaned toward Jamal with grave intent. "When you take the TV license money from the customer, Jamal, who do you give it to?" He articulated each word, surrounding it, for emphasis, with a slight pause.

"I give it to Ronny. Then he goes to the post office and takes out the license."

"I see," replied Mr. Sher. "I wonder whether either of you might explain how fifteen hundred rand's worth of licenses are missing."

At this point Louise had interjected. "Harry, are you accusing my husband? He wouldn't do anything like that. We don't need the money. We're not short of anything. We've got our own money."

Jamal watched as Mr. Sher let Louise finish before turning towards Ronny with barely disguised contempt. "Don't tell me you have your own money. I *know* what you've done."

Unbeknownst to Ronny, a member of staff in the downtown branch had secretly phoned Harry and told him about the suspected missing licenses. When Harry had sent in a customer to take out a TV license as bait, the customer's money was duly taken but the customer was always confronted by excuses whenever he came in to collect his TV license. When Jack had subsequently gone in to check the books, it became evident that their mole was on to something and that this was not an isolated occurrence. More than fifteen hundred rand of license money was missing. For Harry and Jack it wasn't just the money, it was the principle. Besides, if the licensing authorities had discovered the scam before they had—they could have been stripped of their right to sell TVs. It put their company's good name in jeopardy and their livelihood at risk.

Jamal saw Ronny look directly at Mr. Sher, his brown eyes dilating wide as saucers with a kind of hurt pride, and insist, "I don't know anything about the missing license money."

And then he said something that Jamal would never forget: "Why don't you ask Jamal?"

"Yes, maybe it was Jamal," repeated Louise indignantly.

"But, whenever I collect license money," Jamal protested, "I give it to you, in your hands, Ronny."

At that point, Mr. Sher tore into Ronny. "Don't talk a lot of bladdy rubbish," he shouted. "*You* are the manager. *You* must know what happened to the money."

"He's your brother! How can you talk to him that way!" Louise shouted.

"Why are you doing this, Ronny?" Mr. Sher came back at him. "Why are you stooping to this petty theft? What is it with you? Don't you earn enough money?"

Ronny sat there in stony silence.

"If you're not going to come clean," threatened Mr. Sher, "we can call the police. You can explain it to them." Mr. Sher started walking towards the phone in the entrance hall. "Is that what you want me to do? Call the police? The police?"

That was the first time Jamal saw Ronny cry. "I'll never do it again," he wailed. "I swear on my children's lives, I'll never do it again."

Mr. Sher looked at Ronny with withering contempt. He was trembling with anger. "That's what you said last time. That's what you said last time. You can go now. Jack and I will discuss it. We'll let you know tomorrow what we decide."

"Mr. Sher and Mr. Rubin believed I was guilty, too," says Jamal. "Because we were both in positions of responsibility, they held us both liable and made us each pay back half. They deducted seven hundred and fifty rand from my salary. I had not taken any of that license money. I had no part in it. On the way home, Sanji, who had not said a word throughout the meeting, asked me: 'Jamal, did you take the money?' I told her: 'Not one cent.' At that point, hand on heart, I had been honest. I felt very bitter. I hated Ronny for making me pay for what *he* did. I couldn't be angry with Mr. Rubin and Mr. Sher. I knew where they were coming from. I felt lucky to have my job."

For a few months Jamal and Ronny hardly talked to each other. "I couldn't look at him. He couldn't look at me. But as time passed, things eased, our friendship resumed."

Ronny started to confide in Jamal. His daughter had been arrested for tax evasion, he told him. He needed fifteen thousand rand to post bail, and another ten thousand rand to urgently get her out of the country before her case came up again. He was depressed and confused. He would sit and cry at times and worry about his daughter. He was always busy by the safe. "I always wondered why is he taking so long by the safe. One day Ronny called me over and told me how we could steal lots of money. I was scared. I said: 'Won't we get into trouble?'

" 'No one will catch us,' said Ronny.

"Something clicked in my head to say this is extra pocket money for me. Ronny needed the money. I started to feel I needed the money, too. I started to justify it. I thought, if I don't take my share, he'll take it all. That didn't seem fair. Why should Ronny be the only one to live well? This was the new South Africa—I wanted my piece of the pie, too."

Ronny and Jamal began implementing their scheme in 1998. Their plan was simple: whenever they made a big-ticket cash sale—for a TV, or a hi-fi, or a dining room, or bedroom suite—they would divide the cash and pocket it without writing an invoice. They piled the empty boxes of these stock items in the corner of the shop. When Misty, the stock controller, came to take stock once a month, she would holler out the stock item from behind her desk and Jamal or Ronny would simply point to the box and Misty would produce a green tick next to the stock item indicating that it was still in stock. When Misty would go for lunch, Jamal, unable to contain his nervousness, would sometimes surreptitiously tick off in the stock book the items that were no longer in the shop. They were counting on the fact that Misty was lazy and never bothered to actually check inside the boxes herself and that she wouldn't notice the extra ticks made in her absence. Eventually, of course, if they continued to steal the takings of all big-ticket items sold for cash, the shop would have been full to the rafters with empty boxes, but Ronny and Jamal had not thought that far ahead.

Jamal was acutely anxious whenever Misty or Mr. Rubin came to the shop.

"There was no peace in me. Once you get involved in something, it's hard to pull out. I lived and slept with a conscience from that time. Me and Ronny had become partners in crime. Of course, we weren't always honest with each other. Sometimes I made a cash sale and pocketed the money and didn't tell Ronny. Ronny needed the money. But I needed money, too."

Jamal began to develop a taste for a wealthier lifestyle. He told his wife that their newfound prosperity was due to increased sales commissions. He had become a hotshot salesman, he told her, and Mr. Sher and Mr. Rubin were rewarding him handsomely.

"This was the new South Africa. I wanted to live nice, eat nice, dress nice. I became greedy. Once you've crossed the line, it becomes easier and easier to justify. You stop seeing that it's wrong. I felt I got to have *extra* money in my pocket every day."

Harry Sher stands foursquare in front of Jamal, his shoulders hunched, his patience running thin. "I'm not going to ask you again. Does Ronny know anything about it?"

"No," says Jamal. He starts to cry. Tears run down his bony cheeks and splash onto the plastic runner. He does not handle confrontation well. He tries a little lie to elicit sympathy. "I only did it because my wife is ill. I needed the money for her doctors."

"We trusted you," shouts Harry. "And this is how you treat us."

Jack produces a pen and a piece of plain notebook paper and says very calmly. "What we need you to do is write down exactly what you have done and how you did it."

Jamal's hand is shaking. He is thinking, maybe if I cooperate they'll be lenient on me. He writes jerkily:

I, JAMAL SULIMAN, Have Taken Goods From JULES STREET FURNISHERS And Sold For Cash. I Used The Money. This Went On For About A Year. I Was In A Lot Of Financial Problems. I Promise To Pay Back Every Cent I Have Taken From The Company I Have Worked For. I Know I Cannot

Run. I Got To Think Of My Family. What I Have To Say Is Very Difficult. I Am VERY VERY Sorry For What I Have Put Everyone Through. Please, I Don't Want to Lose My Work. I Will Never Think Of Anything Like This Again.

"Now sign it," says Jack.

Jamal is pleading: "Please, please, don't have me locked up. If I go to prison I won't make it. I'm not tough to be in a place like that. They can rape you, they can kill you, they can do anything with you . . ."

"Take him to Jeppe police station," Harry says to Jack. "I want you in jail, Jamal, where the other criminals will *fuck* you. You will wish you had never done this. You'll be better off dead."

CHAPTER 6

The Making of Harry Sher

There are few men who can deliver a soliloquy on the contemporary history of the bed—and elevate it to the realm of social comment on the sexual proclivities of the working classes—but Harry Sher is willing to give it a go.

Until the seventies, he will have you know, there was not much to choose from in the way of beds. There was just the standard rectangular-shaped bed that came in three sizes: the double, the queen, and the king. "The double was very popular with our working class customers. They used to like it, or so they said, because its confined space was a boon to their sex life. By this, they meant that they could, like, *pomp* close-up. You will have to excuse our customers: This is how they talk; they are not exactly the most refined. Be that as it may, beds are important to them. They would spend a lot of time there. In those days, the seventies, most people in Malvern were either sleeping or *pomping* by 9:30 P.M.

"But life got decidedly more interesting when we introduced the avant-garde round bed, called the Athens, in 1975. The Athens was an entirely new concept in beds. For a start, it was extremely eye-catching. It had padded velvet and shiny chintz material all the way around, and it came in a choice of two-toned colors, none of them exactly muted: You could have the glossy pink and gray, or the glossy yellow and black, or the glossy red and black. But not a normal red, I tell you, a neon red. The mattress was set in a rectangular recess cut into a round base, with a round headboard and a round footboard, and covered by a round, glossy bedspread, making the whole thing look round, though technically it was oval.

"Whenever we got a round bed in stock we put it in the front window. Our customers only *smaaked* this bed, especially the ducktail-sporting Afrikaners who lived to the south of the street, the so-called Elvis bohemians. We couldn't stock enough of them. As fast as we bought them, so they crapped out of the store, snapped up like hotcakes. They called it the family bed because, so they claimed, they would roll around on this bed and make their family on it. Others said it wasn't the Athens for nothing—a place to practice your Olympics. We sold those beds for five thousand five hundred rand, which was expensive for those days, especially for our customers. Some of them never took the plastic off. There's something I could never understand. If you ever went to their houses, there is the bed and the lounge suite you sold them six years ago, still with the plastic on.

"Around this time we also started carrying a Scandinavian bed with a mirrored headboard, called the Apollo. It had a cranking device, so you could tilt the bed up or down. The unique selling point of this bed was that you could *watch yourself pomp*. Understandably, this also became very popular with our customers, even though it, too, was expensive. For fifteen years we were the sole distributors of the Apollo and the Athens on the entire length of Jules Street. If you wanted a round bed or a tilting bed you came to us.

"It was one of the things that set us apart from the ten other furniture stores on Jules Street. Everyone else kept roughly the same boring range of beds. Some people would mock our taste, but thirty years later most of those other shops are history, whereas we are still here. The secret to our success is that we have never been afraid to venture, how shall we say, beyond the realms of conservatism. Some would say that we made a virtue out of our own bad taste. We sold things that appealed to our . . . I could almost say sense of humor.

"Rubin and I. We were the display artists. Together we would lay out the store, decide which bed goes here, which bed goes there, and set up the front window. Of the two of us, though, I like to think that I was the artiste; that I had, how shall we say, just a little more flair for design. Style and aesthetics—these are not Rubin's strong points. I understood what our customers liked; I understood their tastes. Gauche, man! Gauche!"

Harry Sher cracks up whenever he thinks of the things their customers go for. He does this seemingly oblivious to his own outlandish dress sense. More than one member of Harry's family is convinced that Harry is color-blind. "It's all orange to him," they say. But Harry prides himself on his unique sartorial style. He always takes pains to show anyone who comments, with a deft lift of his trouser leg: "As long as your socks match your shirt . . ."

Although Harry might playfully mock the people he does business with, he is gifted in his ability to relate to them. His humor and his charisma are powerful tools for communicating with a client base that is barely literate, and his ability to "give it to you straight" is appreciated by most of his staff, who know him as a fair and gener-

ous man. But he is also feared. And though he has mellowed somewhat with age, his temper is legendary. Harry, they will tell you, is
both a man of the people and a man apart.

Harry Sher was born in 1927, the fourth of eight children of Isaac
and Rosie Sher, in Witbank, then a desolate Transvaal town to the
northeast of Johannesburg set among miles of unremittingly flat
corn fields and a coterie of coal mines. Twenty-three years earlier, in
1904, his father, Isaac, had traveled by boat to South Africa from
Shavel, a village in Lithuania. News of the discovery of gold in
Johannesburg in 1886 had trickled through to Eastern Europe, and
for many Lithuanian Jews, weary of the rampant anti-Semitism that
blighted their homeland, South Africa was to become their destina-
tion of choice (in contrast to the Polish Jews who tended to opt for
the United States). Isaac spoke no English when he left Lithuania,
but at eighteen years old, the same age as the adolescent city—Johannesburg—for which he was headed, he had his life before him.

Isaac disembarked at the Cape Town docks and made his way to
the bustling train station at the bottom of Adderley Street. The story
goes that he was desperate for a cup of coffee but did not even have
the four pence to buy one, so the coffee seller, who happened to be a
fellow Lithuanian Jew, made a deal with him. "I will give you a cup
of coffee if you will become my seller," he said. So, forty-five minutes after he disembarked, Isaac had his first job, walking up and
down the platform at the train station vending cups of steaming coffee. The new immigrants were called *greeners*, recalls Harry, and people from the same *shtetl* were called *landsleiters*, and his father told
him that they liked to help each other and stick together.

As soon as Isaac had saved enough money, he caught the train north to Johannesburg where he hoped to gain work through the *landsleiter* network. There a Jewish trader offered him a job as a sales assistant in one of his remote country stores. It meant that Isaac had to travel to a tiny, parched farming town called Frankfort deep in the Orange Free State, a few hours journey by train to the south of Johannesburg. Isaac used to return to Johannesburg once a month to pick up supplies, and it was on one of these trips that he was introduced to Rosie Stein, a short, stocky woman from Fordsburg, one of the earliest—and now poorest—neighborhoods of Johannesburg.

An arranged marriage between Isaac and Rosie followed in 1916, and he took her back with him to Frankfort, where they started a family. But it was not long before the foot-and-mouth outbreak of the 1920s—known locally as the *rinderpest*—bankrupted many of the farmers and devastated the economy of the area. It was time for Isaac and Rosie to move on, and so they moved north, to Witbank, where Isaac learned to mend bicycles and started his own general dealership and bicycle repair business. Within a decade, though, the Great Depression had flattened Isaac, along with the emaciated fields of unpicked corn. For the second time Isaac was bankrupt. So they moved on again, Isaac and Rosie and their burgeoning family of six children, this time to a small town in the Eastern Transvaal called Breyten, strategically placed near a railway junction, the last stop on the line before Swaziland.

Harry, who was eight when his family packed up and moved, remembers his Breyten days as the worst of his life. It was 1935 and the fascism that was beginning to course through Europe found fertile ground in the harsh *platteland* towns of the Transvaal. Breyten had a population of 350 whites (in those days nobody counted the black population), almost all of them Afrikaans, of which just twenty-five—four families—were Jewish. It was the era of the Black Shirts, a simulated South African Nazi party, recalls Harry, and in Breyten these overtly frightening fascists were in the ascendancy. Their influence reached right into the school, where numerous teachers—including Harry's rugby coach—were members. The word *Jood*—Afrikaans for Jew—was regarded as an insult in itself, and Harry was subject to anti-Semitic invective on a daily basis, from teachers and pupils alike.

"One day," recalls Harry, "the rugby coach bellowed out: '*Gee die bladdy Jood die ball,*' which is Afrikaans for 'give the bladdy Jew the ball.' I was so incensed to be called a bladdy Jew by a teacher that when I got the ball I threw it down in disgust and walked off the field. The next day my mother accompanied me to the school intent on *dondering* [hitting] him. She walked up to him, this tiny Jewish woman, reached up on her toes and gave him a *klap* [a smack] across the face. He was over six feet tall and almost as wide, and my mother barely cleared his belly button. 'My child has a name,' she shouted. 'Next time—use it!'

"No doubt," recalls Harry wryly, "he thought a mosquito had bitten him."

The social stigma was made worse by the fact that the Shers were poor. There was always food on the table, but school uniforms were ill-fitting hand-me-downs from the older brothers. "My father couldn't afford to buy me a satchel for my school books, so he gave me his old, heavy gramophone case, which made a loud *clunk* whenever I put it down on my desk. You could die of embarrassment walking to school with a case like that. I remember one day the case fell open with a bang in front of everyone, and the headmaster mockingly declared: "*Hier kom die Jood met die trommel* [Here comes the Jew with the chest]."

But for Harry, even worse than the anti-Semitism he experienced outside the family was the trauma within. Over the years, the marriage between his parents had all but disintegrated. There were not enough bedrooms in their house, so Harry had to sleep in the hallway, and there he would lie awake, unable to sleep, while he listened to his father and mother arguing in the next room. He would often fall asleep to the sound of his mother crying. It's a time Harry won't talk about, a Pandora's box, he says, that cannot be opened.

Some people are crushed by their childhood, but Harry was indelibly made by his. As a result of being treated as inferior—only blacks were lower than Jews in Breyten—came a burning desire to prove himself. As a result of having to defend himself against constant attack came a close-to-the-surface aggression and an adroitness of tongue. And, out of his own strength in adversity came a withering impatience with others who were weak. Harry did not relish being vulnerable, and the armor he would install would ensure he never had to feel vulnerable again.

Stocky and powerful in build, a male version of his mother, and with a rock-hard jaw, Harry's pent-up aggression found a natural outlet in boxing. By the age of fifteen he had become the youth champion of Breyten, and in 1942 his trainer entered him into the Eastern Transvaal Boxing Championships, where he impressively knocked aside all comers on the way to the final. There he came up against a wood carver from Benoni, Vic Toweel, who eight years later, in 1950, would become Bantamweight Champion of the World and go down in the history books as the first South African ever to win a world title.

Harry Sher versus Vic Toweel was a torrid three-round affair. They had fought each other twice before, Harry losing on points the first time, and earning a creditable draw the second. "But this fight I *knew* I had won," recalls Harry. "By the end I was chasing him around the ring, I was landing punches . . . boom . . . boom. . . ." Unfortunately, the judges saw it differently and gave it to Toweel on points. "Hometown decision," quips Harry, seemingly still stung by the perceived injustice. "But," he adds, eyes twinkling, "I am probably the only South African ever to have beaten the crap out of Vic Toweel."

At the end of that year, when Harry was still fifteen, Isaac pulled him out of school so that he could contribute to the family income. Harry was sent to a concession store in a town six miles away. He had no means of transport back home, so at night the proprietor let him sleep in the shop, on a sisal mattress in the glass showcase under the counter. "I have never been so scared in my life," Harry says. "I lay there, as if in a coffin, with rats and mice scuttling around, and only the moonlight to pierce the darkness. *Yusses*, I was *bang* [scared]."

Harry moved on as soon as he could, getting a job with the post office in Carolina, twenty miles from Breyten. There he earned ten pounds a month (South African currency was still pounds and pence), of which he paid four pounds for board and lodging, repatriated two pounds to his parents, and had four pounds left for himself. After passing his postal and telegraph exams, Harry was transferred to the Vryberg post office in the Cape. "In Carolina I was terribly lonely, but in Vryberg I started maturing, emerging from the shell of a withdrawn little Jew boy," he recalls. "It was the first happy period of my life. I learned to dance. I learned to *jol*. I learned to be with the girls."

In 1944, as World War II was drawing to a close, Harry was consumed by a desire to join the armed forces. "Because of what the Germans had done to my people, and because of what had been done to me by the Black Shirts, I had a tremendous need to make a contribution to the war effort." So, in January 1945, at the age of eighteen, Harry joined the South African Air Force. He spent six months training at 64 Air School in Bloemfontein, where he qualified as a radio operator. After completing his air gunnery course in Port Alfred, Harry was all set to fly out to join the troops fighting in Burma when, to his acute disappointment, the war ended.

So Harry returned to civilian life, this time in Johannesburg, where he completed his matric (school-leaving diploma) at night school, and worked during the day as a clerk for the Rand Tobacco Company. During this time Harry became involved in Jewish politics, joining the underground Irgun Movement. When the Israeli War of Independence began in May of 1948, Harry was already part of the Irgun in Johannesburg. Within weeks he was on his way to Israel—along with more than three thousand other volunteers from Canada, Britain, the United States, and South Africa—to make his contribution to the Israeli Air Force (IAF) and what he hoped would be the formation of a Jewish state.

Harry arrived all fired up, only to discover that the newly created IAF had no need for qualified air crew. They had no airstrips and—aside from a motley assortment of prewar Auster and Norseman light aircraft—no modern planes. It was only later that the IAF acquired twenty-five decommissioned German Messerschmitt 109 fighters from Czechoslovakia and three refurbished B-17 Flying Fortress bombers from America. But Harry was undeterred. He volunteered to join the crew of the primitive Norseman as a "bomb-chucker."

Harry recalls his job as follows. "I was in the fuselage with twenty-five bombs lined up in a row in front of me. I had to get down on my hands and knees and wait for the pilot's signal. As we approached the target zone the pilot would give me the thumbs up. He would then bank over the target and, on his next hand signal, I had to pull out the rear pin from each bomb and start rolling them, one by one, out of the door of the plane as fast as I could. Boy, did I roll them. Fast. Like frenzied, man. Pull the pin. Roll. Pull. Roll. The only thing that kept me from falling out of the plane along with the bombs was a canvas harness attached to a crude hook. I was never privy to the targets, but I knew they were somewhere in the Negev desert manned by the Egyptian armed forces. I remember one time we scored a direct hit on an ammunition dump. Man, oh man. It was the finest fireworks spectacle I have ever seen." All in all Harry flew fifteen sorties. The feeling when he returned was "indescribable," he says. "I was on cloud nine. At last I was contributing to something. We were put up in officers quarters. We were the *manne*. The bomb-chuckers were a select crew."

As the war drew to a close, Harry realized that he wanted to become a full-fledged pilot in the IAF. He was accepted for training and flew home to tell his parents, who had since moved to Johannesburg. "But my mother was distraught. All she did was cry. She was convinced that if I became a pilot she would never see me again. And so, with a heavy heart, and out of respect for my mother, I never went back. But I always regretted not becoming a pilot."

Instead, Harry completed a qualification with the Chartered Institute of Secretaries and went to work as company secretary for a crowd called Thompson's Motor Industry, in Selby, downtown Johannesburg. He discovered he had a talent for numbers. Meanwhile, his social life was blooming. The brooding, introverted teenager had become a man of the world, and at the age of twenty-four he met Carmen Rubin. Within twelve months he and Carmen were engaged. It was then that Carmen's father, Max, made Harry a proposition: He asked him whether he wanted to run his bicycle shop on Jules Street.

In 1952 Harry started to manage Jules Street Cycle Works, as it was then called. It was to be ten years before he would be offered a 50 percent share of the equity, at which point Harry added furniture to the mix and changed the name to Jules Street Furnishers. And it would be two more years before Max would withdraw altogether and Harry would be joined in partnership by Carmen's younger brother, Jack.

CHAPTER 7

Detective Inspector Rich Molepo

Detective Inspector Rich Molepo is surprised to see Jamal Suliman in the charge office. He knows Jamal as one of the managers of Jules Street Furnishers in town, a shop situated only a few blocks from the police station, and where he, Rich, has been a customer for five years.

In fact, he has bought most of his household possessions from Jules Street Furnishers—his hi-fi, his television, his double bed, room divider, and cupboards. He still owes a couple of thousand rand on his account, a debt that, truth be told, is some months overdue. Every now and then someone phones from the shop and asks politely when he is coming to pay his account. He usually promises to go in on the weekend, but doesn't always get around to it. Now, as he stands behind the scuffed wooden counter of the scantily furnished charge office, carefully reading, and then rereading, the confession that Jack Rubin has thrust in his hands, he cannot believe what it says.

"We want to lay a charge of theft," says Jack evenly. Jamal is cowering on a low wooden bench in the corner looking deathly pale.

He is reading the posters pasted to the walls that proclaim in bold red type: "Crime kills, crime destroys, crime is a menace, let's CRUSH it!" Another one says: "Zero tolerance on crime in Gauteng."

Molepo takes one look at Jamal and pulls Jack into the corridor for a private conversation. "Mr. Rubin," he says slowly, "I know Jamal. I have been a customer of Jules Street Furnishers for many years. He seems like an honest man to me. Maybe you should give him another chance. You know, handle this internally, by a disciplinary hearing. Do you really want to lay a charge of theft?"

Molepo's desk is already overflowing with more cases than he can cope with. Since 1994 the spiraling rise in crime faced by the Jeppe police station has been unprecedented: Armed robbery cases up 50 percent, fraud up 67 percent. Molepo knows, too, that it's no better elsewhere, that the soaring crime rate in Jeppe is, if anything, mild compared to the city as a whole and to the rest of the country. Just recently the government published the national crime statistics, and stashed somewhere on Molepo's desk is a document that gives the full picture. The highlights of this document are that since the new South Africa began, robbery countrywide has increased by 169 percent, housebreaking by 33 percent, carjacking by 30 percent, cash heists by 30 percent, assault by 30 percent, rape by 25 percent, and indecent assault by 70 percent. Only murder has gone down. But even this piece of relatively good news turns out to be misleading, because political murders between the formerly bitter political rivals, the ANC and Inkatha, were especially high in 1994. All this extra crime but hardly any extra manpower to tackle it, Molepo knows, is not a winning combination.

"He stole a lot of money," says Jack.

"Was it maybe . . . I'm not suggesting . . . but maybe you weren't paying him enough, that he had to steal from you."

"He was getting a good salary," says Jack.

"You know, Mr. Rubin," continues Molepo, straightening his yellow paisley tie and tugging awkwardly on his maroon cardigan, "I take home two thousand rand a month after tax and deductions. I've been in the force since 1979. I can tell you I struggle to come out. Does he earn as much?"

"He earns *twice* as much."

Molepo shakes his head. "Ai-yai-yai! Then there's no excuse."

Molepo leads them at an amble along the two-tone, green-and-gray corridor to a room on the first floor of the three-story Jeppe police station. His small rectangular office, which he shares with another detective, is lit by a strip fluorescent bulb and is sparsely furnished. There are two old wooden desks arranged in an L-shape, piled high with dockets. Balanced in the crack between them is a single telephone, which the detectives must share, that has been blocked from making calls to cell phones or to numbers outside Johannesburg. Along one wall are a couple of dented metal filing cabinets. One of them sports a hanger, and on it Molepo has hung his police uniform: his blue tunic with stars on each shoulder and a badge that says MOLEPO, his hard blue police cap, blue police shirt, blue trousers, and bulletproof vest with POLICE in bold yellow. Today he is not expecting to go out, so he is dressed in a dark suit. He keeps his gun, a Z88 9 mm Parabellum, tucked into his trousers.

Natural light filters in through the blinds and occasionally the room shudders and shakes as a train rumbles by. Through the window Molepo has a partial view of the railway line that runs behind the police station heading south to the John Page bridge, whereupon it crosses Jules Street and swings east, traveling in parallel along the entire length of Jules Street, all the way to Germiston.

Molepo indicates that Jack and Jamal should pull up two chairs. He casts around for a pen and settles into his chair to take their statements. Just then, a svelte young man strolls jauntily into his office. "Meet my partner," says Molepo, his face breaking into a broad grin, and revealing the absence of his two front teeth. "Meet Sergeant Thomas Magubane."

Magubane doffs an imaginary hat and offers Molepo a Rothmans. He perches on his desk and listens as Molepo, smoke now billowing from his nostrils, begins to take statements, first from Mr. Rubin, then from Mr. Suliman.

Molepo works slowly, rubbing his ample forehead whenever they come to a point in the story that mystifies him or requires further explanation. When people first meet Molepo, who is forty-seven, they can sometimes mistake his genial amiability for laziness or slowness. But Molepo prides himself on being thorough. He believes that he is neither especially clever nor stupid, but, like the average man, somewhere in between.

Molepo grew up the youngest of five brothers in Volksrust, a small town in the Transvaal, where his father worked as a laborer on the railways and his mother was a "kitchen girl" working in whites' kitchens. He started school late—at age eight—and finished late, at twenty-two, but, despite his extended years of study, left with a standard eight, two years short of completing his matriculation diploma. That was enough, though, to get him the job he wanted. After a short stint as a railway policeman he became a constable, and then in 1984 he was promoted to sergeant and assigned to the Jeppe police station. There were no further promotions under the apartheid regime, but in 1999 he got his big break: promotion to Detective Inspector, which meant more rank and slightly more money.

As Molepo takes Jamal's fingerprints and fills out the details on Fingerprint Form SAP 76, which he will send to the Criminal Records Centre, he cannot help feeling sorry for Jamal. Now that Mr. Rubin has left, the accused man is slumped over his desk. He has no stomach to arrest this man. And yet, the more he mulls over the details of the story he has just heard, the more he feels sorry for Mr. Rubin, too. This case, he says to himself, is about a breakdown of trust. And trust is the glue that holds everything together. Hadn't he—when he first bought goods on credit from Jules Street Furnishers—trusted them to provide him with genuine bona fide quality brands and deal honestly with his account? And hadn't they—when they asked him what his job was and for whom he was working—trusted him to tell the truth and to pay the money he owed? Which he had done, mainly, and fully intended to do.

In his experience, he reflects, most people commit crimes because they are jobless and hungry. Jamal doesn't fit into this category. Jamal, it seems, has enough for his basic needs, but wants more. More than his employers are prepared to pay. This is something to which Molepo can relate. No one knows better than Rich Molepo the frustration of a piss-poor salary. You live under the boot of apartheid your whole life, and then the new South Africa comes along—and what? Five, six, seven years later, you're still risking your life and working for peanuts. It doesn't surprise Molepo that some of his police colleagues—yes, his colleagues, and not some but many—have started dabbling, for their own gain, in the underworld of crime.

Sometimes he wonders aloud to his partner: What keeps *us* straight? Thomas always insists it has nothing to do with morality. "It is fear, pure and simple," he says. "As breadwinners, we are kept honest because of what might happen to our families if we are caught."

Eventually Molepo looks up from his completed paperwork. "Would you like a cigarette?" he asks Jamal. The two men light up and start to chat.

"Why did you do it?" Molepo asks, leaning back in his chair in a cloud of smoke. Jamal recounts the story of how Ronny Sher, his manager, had showed him how they could steal from their bosses, and how he began to get a taste for the lifestyle.

"Why did you not mention Ronny in your statement?" asks Molepo. "Why have you taken all the blame on yourself?"

Jamal shrugs. "Ronny will help me. He's my friend. He has said he will help me."

Molepo shakes his head. He does not have the heart to tell Jamal that, if convicted, he faces up to five years in prison. Neither does he want to tell him what his fellow prisoners will do to him inside. A person like Jamal—small-boned, soft-spoken, refined will find it very hard to survive.

"You do understand," adds Molepo, ushering Jamal to the door, "the prosecutor will issue a summons for you to appear in court. In the meantime you are free to go."

Jamal shuffles out. He suddenly feels desperately, mind-numbingly exhausted. It has been a long, long day. He just wants to be home, safe, and secure in the soft arms of Sanji. But he is also scared to go home. A process has begun. Wheels are turning. He has a dull sense that his life is no longer his own, and that nothing and no one—not even Sanji—can ever be taken for granted again.

CHAPTER 8

Lunch Time

The weeks before Christmas are the busiest time of year at Jules Street Furnishers. With Jamal's court date set for February, Jack and Harry turn their attention to other things: sprucing up their windows, ordering stock, and enticing new customers into the shop with seasonal specials. Life can get a little hectic in the last few shopping days before Christmas, but at Jules Street Furnishers, one thing remains reassuringly constant: Harry and Jack always make time for lunch.

Every day at 1 P.M. Beauty rattles the slamlock security gate and Harry rises from behind his desk, twirls his heavy bunch of keys around his wrist, and strides down the plastic runner to open up. Usually, though not always, he greets her with a "thank you, Beauty," or he may exchange a few friendly words of greeting in her own language, whereupon she smiles, replies in her own language, and deposits one bent metal tray on Jack's desk and another on Harry's. On each tray, laid out by Beauty on a white plate, is the packed lunch their respective wives have sent in with them, together with a cup of tea.

Harry has his routine: He clears his desktop, spreads open the *Citizen* newspaper, and pulls his plate towards him, reading as he eats. Today, Harry's wife Carmen has made him turkey legs in curry sauce with lettuce and tomato relish. Julia has given Jack an egg mayonnaise roll with salad, a pear, and an apple. Jack pulls his tray towards him, whistling one of his favorite tunes: *When the Saints, oh when the saints, oh when the saints go marching in, I want to be in that number, when the saints go marching in.*

When Harry glances up, he sees Jack leaning back in his seat, toying gingerly with his sandwich. "You know, Rubin," he says, holding up his half-finished turkey leg, "whenever my wife gives me these, you start drooling. Why don't you ask Julia to make some?"

"What? Me tell Julia what *I* want for lunch?" Jack scoffs at the thought. "Sometimes I might venture to say: 'Julia, please don't put so much salad on the roll, it makes it too wet.' Does she listen?"

"Me too," laughs Harry. "Whatever Carmen gives me, *that's* what I have. She's the lunch mafia. And every day when I get home Carmen will ask me: 'How was your lunch, Harry?' It's never, 'How was your day, Harry?' It's always, 'How was your lunch?'"

The two men joust on, their conversation punctuated by the soft flap of the blinds in the summer wind, the barely perceptible hum of the fluorescent lights, and the signature sound of the fax machine as it spews out credit references. Occasionally a dog barks from one of the houses situated behind the high tension barbed wire fencing at the back of the shop.

Their desks, arranged at right angles, are their domains. Harry is a man of meticulous order. There are only a few items on his desktop, and he keeps tidying and sorting them, immediately returning each object to its allotted place after use. To his right he keeps his Casio ticker tape adding machine and his telephone. In a straight row extending east to west across the top of his desk, he keeps an ancient wrought-iron paper punch ("antique," claims Harry, "antiquated," counters Jack), a stapler, a glass paperweight, a rickety in-tray basket, a well-thumbed bank deposit book, a pile of envelopes (full of checks) waiting to be posted and neatly tied in an elastic band, and two pens. When Harry goes home at the end of the day he leaves his desk cleared and pristine. Even his wastepaper basket looks neat and empty.

Jack's desk, on the other hand, has the same low-tech items of equipment as Harry's, but you cannot see any of them, as they are buried under interlocking layers of papers and files. Jack has a system, too, he claims: things to be done today in one pile, things to be done this week in another pile, things to be done long term stuffed in a third pile. And spread across them all, reams of computerized debtors' age-analysis printouts.

"That desk of yours—always a mess!" scoffs Harry.

"The only reason your desk is tidier than mine," counters Jack, "is because you've got less work than me."

"That is one cheap desk you've got, Rubin," says Harry, changing the angle of attack. "Pure chipboard."

Jack pulls out the drawers as if to examine them. "No Sher, this is solid mahogany. No chipboard here."

"Chipboard, man!" mocks Harry, snorting with laughter.

"I don't know why *you're* laughing. You act like yours is teak. Yours is imbuia."

"Imbuia? Imbuia!" Harry stands up and circles Jack's desk, inspecting it from all sides.

"The whole thing is chipboard, man. Oh, Rubin . . ."

Jack is laughing, his ears reddening. "Mahogany, I tell you."

"Chipboard!" Harry guffaws. "Now mine, on the other hand," he strokes his desk affectionately, "mine is teak."

To the observer the two desks appear identical: Both are made of dark brown wood, both are scuffed and well used, and both have tan leather inlays on the desktop that look fake. What's more, both men acquired their desks from their respective sons. Harry got his when his son moved to New York twenty years ago; Jack inherited his when his son left for London fifteen years ago. The similarities are more striking than the differences, but to Harry and Jack, who has the "cheaper" desk is an endless source of entertainment.

Every room tells a story and this one more than most. At first glance, it looks like the kind of office you might find in a factory or a warehouse. There is no pretension about it, no color scheme, no sense of aesthetic or comfort. The once-white walls are for the most part bare, decorated here and there with freebies or other people's castaways. A calendar from Dreyer & Stratham, the duvet and blanket suppliers, hangs off-center on a nail behind Harry's desk. Two abstract paintings by Carmen, Harry's wife, brighten the wall opposite Jack's desk. "I think those are two of Carmen's not-so-good ones that nobody wanted," Jack has been known to remark. "Her *early* works." Below the paintings is a trestle table with an old radio, a fax machine, and a broken orange plastic flyswatter.

A worn-through, colorless acrylic cord carpet covers the vinyl floor tiles, and over it a plastic runner carries you halfway across the carpet and then stops, mysteriously, in the middle of the room. In the corner is a musty, walk-in strong room with a four-inch-thick reinforced steel door painted in pale green, matching the pale green of the slamlock security gate. Inside the strong room is a diminutive Chubb safe, where Harry and Jack keep the overnight cash takings, and metal filing cabinets stacked with mobile phones and old ledgers and accounts.

Their office is a purely functional space and has hardly changed in years. Everything—from the paint on the walls to the carpet on the floor—is faded. Only the characters who inhabit it are larger than life.

"We're not trying to impress anyone," says Jack. "This is our private space. It's not as if we have customers up here. No need for *plush*."

Although they demand nothing more than that it should be an unremarkable spartan sanctuary away from the hustle of Jules Street, the office nevertheless holds physical clues to earlier crimes and misadventures, clues that reveal much about the dramatic nature of life on Jules Street. The plastic runner, for example. The plastic runner is an enduring reminder of the legacy of Mel Vos, the motor mechanic who they went into partnership with, briefly, two years ago.

The story goes like this: Mel, one of their Afrikaans customers, who improbably claimed to have once completed a year of medical school, came to them one day with a surefire scheme—He wanted to go into the "immensely profitable" car-rebuilding business. He was looking for a sleeping partner to give him the capital injection to get started, and in return he was offering 50 percent of the profits.

"*Ag, man*, you can make a bladdy killing," Mel told them.

The car rebuilding business was one that Harry and Jack knew nothing about, so Mel explained how it worked: You bought two cars of roughly the same make that had been written off in accidents. Maybe the front of the one car was smashed to pieces but the back was fine, and the back of the second car was smashed to pieces but the front was fine. So you bought each car for next to nothing from the scrap yard, you cut them in half, you welded the good back bit of the first car to the good front bit on the second car, gave it a spray paint, and, hey presto—a new car! "When they are well done you won't even guess it's a rebuild," boasted Mel. "A killing, man; I know blokes who are making a bladdy killing."

Mel already had his eye on a couple of Ford Fiestas, he told them. He could buy them for two grand and sell the rebuild for eight, turning a quick profit of six grand. "So, how about it? You put up the capital, I do the work, and we go fifty-fifty?"

Harry consulted his lawyer son in Manhattan, who warned him, "Don't touch it with a barge pole." Jack spoke to his accountant son in London, who advised him, "Leave it well alone."

But Harry and Jack were tempted and soon they were knee-deep in the rebuilding business. Mel would visit regularly with progress reports, but every time he came he would drip oil and grease onto Harry and Jack's office carpet. It upset Harry to see black splotches staining their carpet, so he told Mel that he must clean himself up before he arrived, or do something to protect their carpet. Mel duly arrived with a plastic runner, which, though not long enough to fully protect the carpet, has been a permanent installation ever since.

Every subsequent time Mel visited he would be ushered down the runner and seated on a brown plastic chair in the middle of it. First he came to tell them about the Fiesta. They had turned a nice profit, he said. But he wanted to keep the money to plough it back into the business. This time he had his eye on a couple of Toyotas. A few weeks later, he trooped down the plastic runner to tell them about the Toyota rebuild. "*Ag*, what a nice little earner that was," he said. Again, he suggested that they plough their share of the profits back into the business. So far, so good.

Mel became bolder. "There's a smashed-up truck," he said. "*Ag*, it's a bladdy steal, man. But I'll need more bucks."

By the time oily Mel had disappeared into thin air—and taken their truck and their capital investment with him—Harry and Jack had lost, by their calculations, exactly ten thousand, five hundred and eight rand, and gained a plastic runner.

"Another one who *stole* from us," Harry and Jack would leer.

More telling, and certainly more frightening, is the story behind the hacked-away brickwork around the ventilation grille high up inside the strong room. If you look closely, it appears as if someone has tried to scrape off the paint work with their bare hands. Behind these markings lies an incident vividly remembered, not least because, in retrospect, it heralded the beginning of a crime wave on Jules Street Furnishers that has never ceased.

It was Saturday, December 5, 1987, just before closing time. Harry was off work that day and Jack had already left for the golf course, so it was left to Fernando Perreira, their Portuguese branch manager, and Suzette Fish, their Afrikaans assistant manager, to lock up the shop.

"That day is, like, *yus* yesterday in my mind," recalls Suzette. "It was ten to one in the afternoon and I went to the big sliding door at the front of the shop to close up, when this man, he comes to the door, and he says he wants to look at the round bed we have on display in the window. I say to him in Zulu, 'Hey, I'm closing up now.' Just quickly, he wants to *boega*, to look, he says. Stupid me, I open the door and as I am straightening the bedspread, he grabs me and spins me around and holds a knife against my throat—one of those jagged-edge blades. He lifts me up and propels me forward towards the back of the shop. I see Fernando reading the newspaper by the cabinets where we keep the cash and I try to attract his attention. Next thing, two more men come running past me, jump the counter, and they've got a gun to Fernando's head. One has his hair in dreadlocks, the other is in a blue overall. The guy who has a knife to my throat throws me in the corner and says, 'Not a word from you. I'll slit your throat. I'll kill you.' I can't speak a word, even if I want to. It is like my voice has just gone. I am a lump of cement. And Fernando—Fernando has gone white as a sheet. He keeps his gun in the bottom drawer, and the cash in the top drawer. The robbers start stuffing their pockets—but there is only about three hundred rand there. They demand that we open the safe upstairs. (Now, how did they know there was a safe upstairs? I am telling you they had inside information—someone on the staff was in on this.) They take me, knife at my throat, and Fernando at gunpoint, up the stairs to the strong room. They seemed to know exactly where it was. Inside, there was a glass cabinet with twenty watches. One robber takes the butt of his gun and smashes the cabinet and scoops up all the watches into a brown paper bag.

"'Where's the money?' he says to Fernando.

" 'There is no more money,' says Fernando. 'Nothing. No more. Just what you took.' The reggae man pushes the gun into Fernando's head. 'If you don't open the Chubb, I shoot you.' "

Fernando picks up the story. "I don't say nothing. I shaking like bladdy mad. I shaking so much I can't fit the key into the door. The guy is shouting: 'Open up or I kill you.' I try and steady my hands and push the key in and turn and just open the bladdy safe. They take the money—a whole week's takings, about sixty thousand rand—and they throw us into the strong room and slam the door. I am sweating. Suzette is sweating too. She is wearing a very thin, see-through blouse and skirt. It is December, very hot. After a while you can see everything. Everything!"

"I hear them turn the key," continues Suzette, "but I don't hear them take the keys out, so I say to Fernando, 'The keys are still in the door.' But already Fernando is starting to get claustrophobic. The strong room is tiny—there's just about one meter square of space for us both to stand in. I say to Fernando, 'Don't panic—my husband is fetching me. He'll be here any minute. They've left the key in the door. Jonny will save us.'"

"Meanwhile, downstairs Jonny has entered the shop. He sees a guy in blue overalls behind the counter. Confused, because he doesn't recognize him, he walks up and asks, 'Where's Missus Fish?'

" 'She's busy upstairs,' he replies. So Jonny is walking around, waiting for Suzette to come back downstairs, when suddenly he feels a gun in his back.

"I am in the safe praying: *Please Lord, let my husband come to my rescue. He's going to save me and Fernando. We won't die in here.* Next thing, the safe door is pulled open and who comes flying in? Jonny.

They just chuck him in. I can't even cry. I am so scared. Then the one in the overall says, 'Shoot the bastards.' And I watch the reggae guy lift his gun and point it at us.

"Fernando goes down on his hands and his knees. 'Please God, don't kill us. Don't kill us. We got families, we got children.'

"Like I say," says Suzette, "I can't speak, I can't speak, but Fernando is on his knees. I see him dip the gun, and I think, here goes. I see my two daughters flash past me. My blood runs cold. He dips the gun, and then he turns away, and the next thing, they have slammed the door and locked us in."

Suzette grabs an old picture frame with a photograph of Jack's father and starts bashing the ceiling, hoping that the people who live in the flats above the shop will hear them. Jonny spots the ventilation grille and starts chopping away at it with his bare hands. If he can open it, they reason, they can shout to people in the houses at the back, and also let in some fresh air. They throw everything—books and files—off the shelves and Jonny starts tearing at the wall.

"You should have seen his fingernails!" exclaims Suzette. "Jonny manages to open the vent a tiny bit, enough to see it only opens onto the bladdy mattress storage room next door. Meanwhile Fernando is on his hands and knees, trying to suck in fresh air under the door. We're all sweating. I know we're going to die."

Suddenly Fernando pulls a pack of Peter Stuyvesant cigarettes and matches from his top pocket. "I know! Let's make a fire!" he shouts.

"Are you bladdy mad?" Jonny shouts back. "Make a fire! You want to burn our last little bit of oxygen? You crazy?"

"No, people will see the fire, man," says Fernando.

"See the fire, your arse. We'll be burnt alive. You bladdy mad!"

Jonny turns his attention to the steel door of the strong room. He twists free a steel bar from the filing cabinet and starts levering away at the screws holding the inside panel in place. Suzette is standing on the table chopping the roof with a piece of wood, screaming and shouting, hoping someone will hear them. The air supply is dwindling and she is convinced they are going to suffocate. Eventually, after two frantic hours, his hands bleeding, Jonny painstakingly manages to prize off all the screws from the inside of the door. He and Fernando pull the inside panel off its hinges, to reveal a further set of metal pins holding the locking mechanism of the door in place. Working feverishly, their air supply thinning noticeably now, they hack out the pins, and as they do so, the whole lock hinge slides back and the door swings open. Fernando falls forward and starts kissing the ground.

"I started blubbing like a bladdy baby," says Fernando. "I'm not cut out for this. I'm a ladies' hairdresser by trade, not a bladdy Rambo."

Fernando's journey from the streets of Lisbon, where he was born, to Jules Street in Johannesburg has been an eventful one. Born in 1937, Fernando came from a family of ladies' hairdressers: his father, mother, two brothers, sister, and himself, "all of us hairdressers," he says proudly. When he was twenty-two Fernando emigrated to Mozambique, seduced by a contract to work as the in-house hairdresser at the Polana Hotel, the most prestigious hotel in what was then Lorenco Marques and is today Maputo, the capital of Mozambique. It was there that Fernando—who is just five feet five inches tall, dark-haired, and rotund—met his wife-to-be, Graca, daughter of a Portuguese lieutenant colonel. Together they would have four children, three boys and a girl.

But when disaster struck Mozambique in the form of torrential rains that became a flood—and the sea-level Polana Hotel, with its ground-floor hairdresser, was shoulder-deep in water—Fernando's hair dryers and expensive equipment, which were uninsured, got destroyed. "I had what you call a nervous breakdown," he says. "The doctor say I was shaking. I could not sleep. I lose everything."

Fernando had a brother-in-law living in South Africa who suggested he come for medical treatment. With the roads flooded, he put his car on a train and headed across the border. Within a week, Fernando was offered a job at John Bar, one of the largest hairdresser chains in the country. He sent for Graca and the kids.

It was 1963. Fernando was much in demand, but he had a problem: he didn't speak a word of English. "Not even I can say thank you," he says. "In fact, my English is so bad at that time that I want to fire one of my hairdressers working for me, and the next day she comes and thanks me for the raise. I thought I had 'fired' her, because she was so useless, but apparently what I told her was that I had 'highered' her [salary]. My wife had to explain and break the bad news."

To cut a long story short, after a number of jobs, Fernando became the in-house hairdresser at OK Bazaars in Eloff Street in downtown Johannesburg. Fast-forward to 1978, a bad year for hairdressers. "That was the year the blow-wave start in South Africa," recalls Fernando. "You lose time drying, drying, drying. Everything take longer. Business not good. So I resign as hairdresser and start to work for OK Bazaars as a furniture salesman. One day Mr. Rubin come into the shop and see what a good salesman I am and invite me to join Jules Street Furnishers. It was 1981 and a lot of Portuguese people were living around Jules Street, and they were looking for someone who could attract Portuguese customers into the shop."

It took Fernando two years to decide. He joined as manager in 1983, and later he was promoted to buyer for the whole group. "When I joined, the crime situation was not bad. In fact, it was nothing. We not even have gates on the windows. But since that day in 1987 it all changed. And it gets worse every year. More and more violent. Holdups, robberies. Commonplace. Now I carry a gun, a 9 mm. It's become frightening. Much safer to be a hairdresser. Do I feel safe in Jules Street? Not since that day. Not at all."

When the safe door fell open, Suzette's whole body was shaking. "I couldn't talk. Fernando was kissing the floor and I was going hysterical," she says.

Jonny telephoned Mr. Sher, who called the cops and an ambulance, and when they arrived, they had to give Suzette a sedative. "Mr. Sher drove me home," Suzette recalls, "while Jonny and Fernando went for a *dop*—a triple brandy and Coke—at a local hotel."

The next day, December 6, 1987, the Johannesburg *Sunday Times* ran the story. "Ingenuity saves trio from death. . . . Two men and a woman escaped death by suffocation after being locked in a safe by a gang of robbers at the weekend," the piece began. They published a photograph of Fernando and Suzette in the safe, and the newspaper complimented them on their "MacGyver-like" ingenuity in fashioning their own escape. "Cleveland police are investigating the incident," they concluded.

"They never caught nobody," says Fernando. "A white policeman came round the next day with millions of photos of blacks. 'Was it *him?* Or *him?* Or *him?*' I couldn't recognize anybody. We told them that the robbers knew exactly where the safe was, that maybe a member of staff had been a secret accomplice, and that they might pursue that line of inquiry. They didn't bother. We never saw that policeman again."

Suzette was too afraid to return to work. "Don't go back, it's not safe on that street anymore," Jonny said. "It's not like the old days when you used to *jol* down Jules Street like Zorro."

Suzette often talked about gamboling in Jules Street as a kid. She was born in 1950, the third of five children, in a semidetached house just a few blocks from the premises of Jules Street Furnishers. Suzette's father operated the elevator at nearby City Deep gold mine before contracting tuberculosis from the damp, foul air down the mine and having to take early retirement. Many of the people who lived on Jules Street back then were white mining families, like themselves, who rented houses owned by the mines. The single black men who worked the mines alongside them were prevented from living on the street, and were billeted instead in crowded compounds on the far edges of the mine's property. In the fifties, as Suzette recalls, Jules Street was a safe, quiet, white world. The tram ran straight as a javelin down the center of the street, all the way from town, made a U-turn at the end of Jules Street, and then trundled back on itself, ringing its brass bell as it went. She remembered how she and her friends used to leap on and off the tram platform, which was situated directly opposite the premises of Jules Street Furnishers, and pretend they were Zorro.

Suzette's first memory of Mr. Sher goes back to when she was a child. Her parents used to buy groceries "on tick" (buy now, pay at the end of the month) from *ou* (old) Mr. Rubin, Jack's father, who owned a grocery store called B.W. Becker, on the corner, as well as a tiny bicycle shop next door, which by then was being run by Mr. Sher. "Mr. Sher knew me from when I was just out of the pram," laughs Suzette. "Me and my brothers, we bought our first bikes from them." Later, when Suzette married Jonny, they bought their furniture from Mr. Sher and Mr. Rubin, including their double bed.

"*Ya*, we made our whole *jurra* family on that bed," she grins.

Later, as a young mother, walking her two daughters to school, Suzette would pass Jules Street Furnishers and stop for a chat. In those days, Mr. Sher and Mr. Rubin used to stand behind the counter and do everything: sell, take money, write credit agreements. One day, when Jonny had stopped by to pay the account, Harry asked him, "What is Suzette doing these days? Does she want a job?"

"She knows *niks* [nothing] about office work," Jonny replied.

"Man, bring her in. If she wants work, we'll teach her," said Harry.

"That was twenty years ago," recalls Suzette. She started as a receptionist, was promoted to credit controller, then assistant manager and in 1999 became a manager. "They taught me everything," she says. "Those two men have been like second fathers to me."

But they couldn't be more different, she adds. "Mr. Sher, he's very direct, very stern, but always very fair. When he speaks to you, *jong*, he means what he says. He can be hard to communicate with. Like an authority figure. When you have done something wrong, he goes off, he lets you know *jong*. Man! I've seen him take off at a customer built like a ten-ton truck who was going *warra warra* with his big mouth, and Mr. Sher, short as he is, went round the counter and grabbed him by his shirt and said, 'Out of my shop now! Out! Now!' And he dragged him to the front door.

"I've always looked to Mr. Sher as a father. You know, I even tried to hide from him that I smoked. One day I made a slip up and I left my smokes on my desk and he asked the staff, 'Whose are those ciggies?' I would never puff in front of my parents and I would never puff in front of Mr. Sher. Ever since he found out I smoke, I've been doing my utmost to stop. And I'm a fifty-year-old woman! *God*— that's what I mean about a father image.

"Mr. Rubin is, like, the same," continues Suzette, "but I don't look to him as a father. He's more a friend. You can sit down and have a *lekker* conversation with Mr. Rubin. Okay, he's my boss, my superior, but you can relate to him more easy-like. He handles people in a completely different way than Mr. Sher. Once this huge, fat, tub-of-lard customer, a miner if I remember right, came in, all red-faced and pissed off and threw a telegram in Mr. Rubin's face. 'What's this rubbish about you coming to repossess?' Now, Mr. Rubin is a very calm man. He just stood up and checked him out. He never screams, never shouts, he always likes to communicate. 'Let's take a look at your account,' he said. 'See here—this is when you last paid. You are five months overdue. Why don't you at least come in and tell us that you can't pay? That you need time?' By the end, Mr. Rubin had this angry customer from Simmer & Jack gold mine emptying his wallet and licking out of his hand like a puppy dog.

"Sometimes there was tension between Mr. Rubin and Mr. Sher. You could *feel* it, man. Then I used to know I must just zip it. But it wasn't often. It was more jokes. Laughing. *Ag lekker, man.* Fun, fun. When the sales reps used to come in, they used to treat them like family. Mr. Sher and Mr. Rubin used to sit and listen while these salesmen told them the story of their life. Like Rita Badenhorst, she was only a character, *hey*. She would walk in with her bare feet, swaying her hips. She became a loyal customer. *Ag ya* . . . but eventually we had to repossess all her furniture."

Jules Street has changed since those days, says Suzette. "Things were calmer then, clearer, you knew where you stood. Now, there's a shebeen on every corner. The music—*doef, doef, doef*—goes all day. What a racket. You can hardly hear yourself think. After Fernando and I were locked in the safe, I wanted to give up my job. I was a wreck. Finished. A candidate for the asylum. But I decided to go back, because deep down I felt a responsibility to Mr. Sher and Mr. Rubin. Besides, life goes on. You can't run away. After that, for a while, every time a black male customer came into the shop I felt this fear grab my throat. It's horrible to live that way. I have never been racist. It's true, I used to support the old Nationalist Party, and they were racist, like one hundred percent, *jong,* but I only voted for them out of respect for my husband. He was a racist. He would admit that. Although, since the new South Africa he's changed his views. To some extent. Me? I've always tried to treat everybody the same. I didn't like feeling suspicious of customers because of their color. And also, I didn't like feeling unsafe in my job. But we are human beings and we adjust. It's sad to say, but so many things have happened since we were locked in the safe that I have adjusted to always never feeling safe."

Not long after that, Jules Street Furnishers was held up again. This time Suzette was out on an errand buying spray paint for the window display. When she returned, she saw Mr. Sher running out of the shop without his shirt, his face covered in blood. She learned later that the armed robber, who had been wielding a knife, had grabbed Mr. Sher by the collar, but that Mr. Sher had ducked out and run off, leaving the robber holding his shirt. The robber then quickly made his escape. When Suzette got back to her desk, she saw that Fernando seemed to be in some sort of catatonic state. "You've heard of the phrase 'scared stiff'?" says Suzette. "Well, that was how I found Fernando."

"I have this gold wedding band on my finger," Fernando explains. "It's been on my finger forty years, so long now that it's stuck and can't come off. When they held us up one terrible thought went through my head: they would cut off my finger to take my gold ring." He gives a relieved smile. "Thank goodness Harry scared them off and they ran out the shop."

Fernando wears so much jewelry, he literally *clinks* as he walks. He sports a gold Lanco watch, two chunky gold rings with diamonds on his right hand, another two gold rings on his left, a silver wrist bracelet, and a solid gold chain around his neck. "Porra gold!" he says, grinning proudly.

Harry and Jack responded to the holdups by upgrading their security. They installed burglar proofing on the windows and employed security guards at the entrance.

The world had changed since the day, fifty years ago—so Rubin family folklore has it—when a manager absentmindedly left the door of the selfsame shop wide open and had gone home without locking up. Nothing had been taken. Nothing had been in the least disturbed.

CHAPTER 9

Early Days on Jules Street

Jack Rubin can trace his family history on Jules Street back to 1911, the year his grandfather, B. W. Becker, then in his twenties, emigrated from the Hungarian section of Mea Sharim in Jerusalem, Palestine, in search of a climate more conducive to his gangrenous foot. The doctors in Jerusalem had told Barney Walter Becker that his foot was for the chop, that there was no saving it. But B. W. was stubborn. News had reached Palestine that Johannesburg was the fastest-growing town on earth, where men could make fast fortunes on the back of the richest gold rush in history. Unlike most other immigrants who were lured by potential riches, B. W. went for the weather. The highveld summers, he had been told, were unspeakably sublime, the fall and the spring barely perceptible interludes, and the winters were said to be surprisingly mild, with dazzling, azure midday skies that became nippy only towards evening. So he scooped up his family—his wife, Bertha, and their three young children, Bert, seven, Fay, five, and Ruth, three—and hopped on the boat for South Africa.

The Johannesburg that greeted B. W. Becker in 1911 was a town on steroids. In just twenty-five years it had been transformed from a vast, entirely treeless grassveld, populated by a few farmers, to an awesome metropolis-in-the-making, with a quarter of a million inhabitants. The tented diggers' camp of 1886—the year Johannesburg was founded—had quickly given way to corrugated iron shacks, replaced in turn by tens of thousands of brick homes. In the middle of town, ornate buildings—boasting fine wrought iron lacework and balconies, and built of concrete and iron on the Manhattan model—pushed skywards, giving the city an almost instantaneous sense of bustle and grandeur.

By 1911, the gold fields wreathing Johannesburg were already producing an impressive 40 percent of the world's gold. On the back of such stupendous growth, Johannesburg had supplanted every other South African city in importance and had become the social and economic powerhouse at the core of the Union of South Africa, a position it would never relinquish. Its infrastructure was already well developed: there were banks, numerous newspapers, a railway, and a stock exchange. The streets were lined with hundreds of bawdy saloons, drinking dens, and cheap hotels where barmaids turned tricks for thirsty miners—the majority of them single— seeking relief after a long day spent underground. Vice and raunchy entertainment was a distinctive hallmark of early Johannesburg, and there was an abundance of regular theaters and bioscopes (cinemas), which were even more numerous then than today. *The Merchant of Venice* was playing nightly at His Majesty's Theater in Commissioner Street—"starring Matheson Lang as Shylock and Miss Hutin Britton as Portia"—and at the bioscope, the Queen's Coronation was a great favorite. Although Johannesburg would only be accorded official city status in 1928, by 1911 it already boasted the largest urban concentration in South Africa.

The vehicular traffic was something to behold: Horses, bicycles, motorcars, horse-drawn carriages, and double-decker electric trams all vied for the road. Already it was claimed that Johannesburg had more motorcars than any other city of similar size in the world. The town center however, was ill equipped to cope. It had been laid out as a grid, but the blocks were far too short to accommodate traffic flow. When the city was originally planned in 1886, President Paul Kruger had overruled the surveyors and halved the length of the blocks. He apparently calculated that, by doing so, the number of corner properties would increase, and since they were more highly valued than the others, this would boost government coffers when the land was leased or sold. While Kruger's folly contributed to the hurly-burly of the city, making it seem even more intimate and compact, it also caused acute traffic congestion the likes of which would one day contribute to the decline of the city center.

Into this cauldron of helter-skelter development poured immigrants from all over the world. The census of 1910 recorded that the town's population of 237,000 was evenly split between black and white. Of the city's white burghers, 40 percent were English-speaking arrivals from the Cape and Natal, 25 percent were Afrikaans, and the remaining 35 percent were immigrants.

Of these immigrants, a surprising number—like B. W. and Bertha Becker—were Jews. As early as the 1890 census, four years after Johannesburg was formed, 6,253 of the white population—more than 10 percent—had described themselves as Jewish. The high visibility of "Hebrews," as they were called, prompted newspapers to occasionally, and facetiously, refer to the town as Jewburg.

But the Afrikaans population was deeply xenophobic and this was an ever-present fear for the early Jews of Johannesburg. In 1892, President Paul Kruger revealed the depth of his understanding of his semitic brethren when, on being asked to open the very first synagogue in De Villiers Street, he declared, "I open this synagogue in the name of our Lord Jesus Christ."

B. W.'s first challenge was of a practical nature: to find work and a place to live. By 1911, as he was to discover, the geography of Johannesburg already reflected its race and class divisions. On the west side of town were the clearly demarcated "Coolie," "Kafir," and "native" locations, as they were called, where many of the town's Indians and blacks lived in appalling poverty. To the north was a rocky outcrop called Parktown Ridge, where the plots were large, the air clear, and the outlook superb; and there lived the white property magnates and mine owners—called randlords—whose ostentation would become the stuff of legend. The French randlord Jacques Lebaudy had famously installed a swimming pool that he filled with champagne. The high-society dame Lady Dale Lace was chauffeured around in a carriage pulled by trotting zebras.

Between these two extremes—squander to the north and squalor to the west—lay the working-class east. It was there that new white immigrants such as B. W. Becker were initially directed.

In fact, the very first instincts of the town had been eastward. The impetus driving development was the gold mines, studded across the veld to the south of town on an east-west axis. To the east of the town center, in the suburbs of Jeppestown, Belgravia, and Troyeville, lived the working-class white miners, close to the point of production and close to the town center. Interspersed among them was a growing population of artisans, craftsmen, and shopkeepers who made their living catering mainly to the commercial needs of the miners, and not just the whites, but also the migrant blacks who lived in fenced-off compounds on the mine properties. These eastern working-class suburbs, B. W. had heard, were not only accessible, but affordable.

Early one morning, so the story goes, B. W. made a fateful journey that was to lead directly to Jack Rubin and Harry Sher's destiny on Jules Street. B. W. took the double-decker electric tram from the downtown terminus to the eastern suburbs in order to see for himself what opportunities existed. The tram traveled east on Main Street before turning south along Berg Street, and then swung east again, emerging onto a street as long and straight as the eye could see. From the open windows of the top deck, B. W. would have been able to see the golden yellow-white mine dumps to the south of the street, symbols of the city's wealth. They signaled the gold mines of City Deep, Heriot, Jumpers, Stanhope, and Simmer and Jack, their distinctive headgear rising high above the mine shafts and silhouetted against the metallic early morning sky. At this time of day tendrils of steam curled around the base of the headgear, as hot air rising from the underground tunnels hit a thick blanket of cool air still waiting to be warmed by the pale morning sun. The main reef outcrop broke ground just a few hundred yards south of the street, sloping away to the south at a steep forty-five-degree angle. In later years, when the place was all built up, some people would claim that there was gold under Jules Street, but you wouldn't make that mistake back then. Back then you could see quite clearly where the reef ended and the street began.

When the tram reached Belgravia, the driver rang his bell to indicate the end of the line. Looking east, away from town, down the long, straight street, B. W. observed the feverish beginnings of a new suburb. There were no traffic lights in this part of the street, but brown wooden poles, standing tall and erect above the wattle and bluegum trees, carried electricity to the newly painted houses. These houses were laid out cheek by jowl, each with identical tiny balconies and postage-stamp gardens. Many were still under construction. B. W. saw more mining headgear to the south of the street and more houses to the north, but observed few shops.

He set off at a brisk walk, following the tramline that was still under construction. A sign, neat white lettering on blue enamel, alerted him to the fact that he was now entering the newly pro-claimed suburb of Malvern. As he made his way, B. W. fell into step with one of the foremen who was carrying out a safety check on the partially completed tram track. A plan to extend the tram line the full length of the street had been passed by the Johannesburg Town Council in 1904, the foreman told him, and now, seven years later, it was almost complete. Soon, maybe next year, it would open for pas-sengers.

Looking back towards town down the long, straight street, almost six kilometers away in the distance, B. W. could make out the skyline against the ochre sky. Such a street B. W. had never seen. Out here the air seemed fresher, there was open space, verdant parks, elevated picnic spots, paddocks with horses, and, above all, modestly priced houses. When the tramline opened the following year, it would put the eastern reaches of the street within an easy commute of town. People would start to move in. A man who positioned him-self well could make a living.

"Can you tell me," he asked the foreman, "where exactly will the terminus be?"

By the time B. W. got back to Bertha and his children in town, it was dark. "Where have you been?" Bertha wanted to know. He had much to tell her. There was only one thing: He'd forgotten to ask the name of the street.

Jules Street is named after one of the famous early settlers of Johannesburg, Julius Jeppe. The street traces its origins back to 1888, the date of the proclamation of Jeppestown, the suburb through which it makes the first part of its arrow-like journey. As was then the custom, Jeppestown takes its name directly from the surname of the head of the family that founded it, namely Julius Jeppe Senior. Jules Street, on the other hand, is named not after the father, but after the first name of his identically named son, Julius Jeppe, later Sir Julius Jeppe. The family (which included another son, Carl) had emigrated from Germany to South Africa in 1870 and had become land developers, leasing land on the sprawling farm of Doornfontein to the east of the town center. Apart from his wheeling and dealing, Sir Julius Jeppe was to become well known in his lifetime for his pioneering civic work, including being a founder member of the Witwatersrand Agricultural Society, a founder member of the Jockey Club, chairman of the Hospital Board, and the chairman of Lord Milner's appointed Johannesburg town council.

Jules Street emerges soon after March 14, 1888, when the first four hundred stands of a new development on Doornfontein farm were put up for auction, and the first streets—then little more than wagon tracks in the veld—were laid out. These stands were snapped up by the city's mining magnates and subdivided into small one-eighth-acre lots, on which they built cottages that they leased at subsidized rentals to white miners. The area was designated for mixed zoning: "Suitable for business and residential purposes." The only restriction was that they could not be occupied by blacks as principals. Consequently, this initial stretch of Jules Street became a diverse panoply of shops, bars, cottages, and artisan workshops—all exclusively white-owned and occupied.

The circular route traveled by Johannesburg's first-ever horse-drawn tram in 1891 was noticeable for its inclusion of Jeppestown, indicating the importance of the eastern suburbs within the early life of Johannesburg. By 1894, Jeppestown was reported as boasting 421 buildings, including two churches, a Masonic Temple, a library, police barracks, club house, two parks, and a school, St. Mary's Collegiate for girls, much of it along Jules Street.

On January 29, 1897, nine years after the suburb's proclamation, *The Standard and Diggers' News* published an editorial hailing the arrival of Jeppestown.

Of the neat little suburbs wherewith the outskirts of the town proper are studded, Jeppestown may claim to be the most ambitious and to betray the liveliest and most active interest in its own material comfort. The habitable qualities of the eastern environs compare favourably with patrician Doornfontein, rural Booysens, and loyal if grimy Fordsburg, and the habitableness of the ward is no doubt traceable to the good men of Jeppe's being much devoted to home duties and pleasures and domesticated in disposition; or is it that the suburb numbers among its residents more than the ordinary share of citizens who take a lively and heart-whole interest in the affairs of the parish? Be that as it may, as a residential suburb for the man of limited purse, Jeppe's stands unrivaled; its dwellings are compact and comfortable, its roads are things of beauty, it boasts two public parks, it is graced with a railway station, it has been endowed with a post office—to say nothing of a police station—it possesses masonic and other halls innumerable; indeed, it is in very fact only describable as the Eden City of *Martin Chuzzlewit*'s dreams.

Although the report read like a gushing advertorial, parts of Jules Street and Jeppestown were indeed highly sought after. Some of the first randlords, including Sir Julius Jeppe himself, resided in Belgravia—otherwise known as Jeppestown Extension, an almost rural suburb on its eastern rim. Sir Julius Jeppe lived in a magnificent mansion called Friedenheim, a double-story house the size of a hotel, with ornate turrets and pillars, fine wrought-iron lacework, wraparound balconies, and half a dozen chimneys. It was surrounded by verdant gardens the size of parks, replete with fountains, lawns, and landscaped flower beds. On weekends the eligible ladies of the town, draped in flowing gowns and sporting hats plumed with ostrich feathers, would parade down Jules Street and Marshall Street as they made their way to the elegant garden parties at the Jeppe mansion. For a brief period, before the flight of the well-to-do classes over the Parktown Ridge to the northern suburbs beyond, Belgravia was the most fashionable suburb in Johannesburg.

Further development followed in 1904, when Jules Street was extended east into the newly proclaimed suburb of Malvern, which was to be laid out by Ewan Curry, perhaps the best known surveyor of the time. *The Transvaal Critic* of February 16, 1906, greeted the imminent auction of the first eighteen hundred stands with the following editorial comment:

During the past few years the growth and development of townships in the immediate vicinity of Johannesburg has proceeded at a brisk pace, but in no direction have these extensions been so rapid and numerous as in the Eastern Suburbs. Jeppestown has become a thriving business centre, the one time lonely plantations and drives of Belgravia now abound with villa residences, while houses and shops have sprung up in all directions in the adjacent properties. . . . The demand for residential and business sites in this direction still continues, however, and an opportunity is about to be offered to those who wish to acquire stands by the sale of Malvern Township. All residents of the Eastern Suburbs are fully acquainted with the position and possibilities of this new township as it is a popular resort on Sundays and holidays, when hundreds of persons promenade the riding ground from whence an excellent view of the surrounding country can be obtained in all directions. . . .

As the plans of the property show . . . the electric tram is to run through the main street [Jules Street], the rails being already laid, this bringing Malvern within a few minutes journey of the Market Square. In addition to this, Cleveland and Denver [railway] stations are practically on the property, so that the new township enjoys greater facilities of access to the centre of the city than any other suburb. The terms of payment are easy and may be extended over sixteen months with the right of conversion into the freehold at from £75 per stand.

At the time, Johannesburg was under the control of Lord Milner, following the British victory in the Anglo–Boer war of 1899–1902, and the English influence translated into the naming of many of the newly laid out Malvern streets. So it was that the streets parallel to Jules Street on the north side were named after famous British horses that had won the Grand National or the Derby, giving rise to Persimmon Street, St. Frusquin Street, St. Amant Street, Galteemore Street, and Ambush Street. The name of the suburb also had an English flavor: "Malvern," it was noted, was said to be the "healthiest pleasure resort [spa town] in all of England."

By the time B. W. Becker arrived, Jules Street had become the main artery between Johannesburg and the eastern mining towns of Germiston and Springs. The only other road that connected Johannesburg to the burgeoning East Rand was the Main Reef Road, a twisty, grimy single-lane carriage-way full of potholes and traveled daily by heavily laden mining vehicles that crawled along at a snail's pace.

Compared to the Main Reef Road, Jules Street—straight, wide, and true, and with a tram running down the middle—was a road for kings.

Within months of B. W.'s fortuitous tram journey, he had opened a corner grocery shop directly opposite the terminus—which was then still under construction—at the eastern end of Jules Street. He sold dry goods—bully beef, sardines, pilchards, cakes, biscuits, and cigarettes—to a clientele comprised mainly of working class white and black miners. As was then the custom, he named the shop after himself, calling it "B. W. Becker."

Physically, it was not much to look at. It had a red tin roof, white stucco ceilings, and a toilet in the backyard. A small, gabled two-bedroom house attached at the rear provided the family with cramped accommodation. Over the road there was a café and tea-room that opened onto a stable and paddock with half a dozen horses. Alongside the tearoom was a pair of semidetached single-story houses: The Livingston family lived in one, the Muller family in the other. B. W.'s side of the street was entirely residential, except for the two corner properties: B. W. Becker on the one corner, and another grocer, Marks—their competition—on the other.

B. W.'s foot (minus a gangrenous toe that could not be saved) healed nicely in the dry heat of the highveld sun. But the weather turned out to be more volatile than he had bargained for. On many a baking-hot summer afternoon, around 4 P.M., black storm clouds would come racing in like herds of wildebeests, the world would go dark, and high-voltage cracks of thunder and lightning would split the sky. Torrential sheets of rain, often followed by hail almost the size of snooker balls, would pelt down, backing up the storm-water drains and creating instant rivers along Jules Street. Though awe-some in their power, the highveld storms also provided relief from the stifling heat, and cleansed the air of the acidic dust that swirled in off the nearby mine dumps. They were also mercifully short. Within forty-five minutes, the wildebeests had moved on, the sun was blazing, the air fresh, and the light along Jules Street was new and beautiful.

In 1914, amidst mild fanfare, the Malvern tramline finally opened for passengers. The tram driver, Bill Horsman—standing straight as a lamppost in his immaculate uniform with shiny brass buttons and a stiff white cap, and ringing the tram bell to signal their arrival at the terminus—became one of B. W.'s loyal cus-tomers. Elsewhere, the world was going to war, but for the new resi-dents at the far end of Jules Street, things were looking up.

Meanwhile, Bertha had given birth to their fourth child, a chubby daughter called Annie.

A plan had come together. B. W. put up a brass plaque at the front of his shop (a plaque still there to this day). It said: "Here since 1911."

When B. W.'s two eldest daughters, Fay and Ruth, were barely out of their teens, they took a vacation to the emerging seaside resort of Durban. There they met a young man, Max Rubin, who, like their father, had emigrated from Palestine.

Max Rubin was an agronomist who had studied at Mikva Yisroel, a renowned agricultural school founded by the British Rothschild family and situated along the road between Jaffa and Jerusalem. After qualifying, Max had decided to follow his older brother to South Africa, getting a job with the Slezingers, the Jewish farming family who owned the Zebediela Citrus Estate in the northeastern Transvaal, then reputed to be the largest orange plantation in the southern hemisphere. Max was an extrovert and handsome, with a naturally toned physique, a beaming smile, and a big personality.

It was at the annual Palestine Society dinner dance in Durban that Max made the acquaintance of the Becker sisters. They could converse in Hebrew, a huge relief to Max, whose rustic English hardly extended beyond a few basic words. Over the following days, Max spent time with the Becker sisters, going for lazy walks along the promenade, swimming in the warm Indian Ocean. Soon Max found himself falling for Ruth, a husky-voiced brunette whose vivacious personality gelled with his own. He appreciated the qualities of Fay, a straight shooter who was always honest and direct; but Fay was the more awkward-looking, with wiry hair, and her introvert personality was less appealing to him. However, the sisters were chaperones for each other, and so, being a gentleman, Max spent the rest of his vacation escorting both Becker sisters about town. He would have to wait until the appropriate time to make his feelings known.

When Max returned to his farm in the northeastern Transvaal, he began corresponding with the woman he hoped would become his wife. Hebrew-English dictionary at his side, he wrote her a long letter, openly declaring his love for her, and asking her to write back. Back on Jules Street, Fay was surprised to find herself the object of Max's writerly affections. She could have sworn that it was her more glamorous sister that he had been after, but no—the letters were addressed to her. "Dear Fay," they began. And they kept coming. Fay wrote back, tentatively at first, but when Max kept corresponding, his joie de vivre flying off the pages, she became bolder. The two of them became regular and intimate correspondents.

But Max had made an almost biblical mistake: On return to Zebediela, he had transposed the names Ruth and Fay. The letters he wrote were addressed to Fay, but the face in his mind was that of Ruth. For months, Max corresponded with Fay, all the while thinking he was writing to Ruth.

It was a year before Max discovered his error. He arrived one afternoon in downtown Johannesburg, jumped on a tram to Jules Street, and there, as arranged, waiting to meet him out front of the dusty corner store, B. W. Becker, was a bright-eyed Fay Becker. Max embraced Fay warmly. "It's good to see you," he said emphatically. Max was always emphatic when he was feeling happy.

And then, politely, he inquired: "Now, where is your sister?" But as Max was about to discover, Ruth was already spoken for, engaged to another man.

Max swallowed his crushing disappointment and said nothing of the embarrassing mix-up. At the same time he began to reason that perhaps he was meant to be with Fay. Their regular correspondence had brought him closer than he had ever been to a woman—and so a few months later, he proposed.

At the beginning of the thirties, the Great Depression took Johannesburg in its clammy grip. Long queues of hungry, jobless people would form outside B. W.'s shop. "People were struggling with their personal hygiene, their hair so infested with lice that you could practically see the critters jumping from head to head," recalls one now elderly, former customer. Every day, B. W. would hand out free food—butter, eggs, flour, tinned fruit—to the starving blacks and whites of Jules Street. It was a daily act of compassion that his customers and fellow shopkeepers would remember, and talk about, for years to come. But what they didn't know was that B. W., then just forty-five, understood what it felt like to be vulnerable. He was dying, the doctors had told him, of tuberculosis.

Before 1931 was out, B. W. Becker had passed away, Bertha had returned to Palestine accompanied by her youngest daughter, Annie, and in accordance with B. W.'s wishes, Fay and Max Rubin inherited the grocery shop.

From the beginning, Max had no particular liking for the retail business. But needing to make a living for his young family—Fay had already given birth to their first child, Carmen—he knuckled down. Besides, he was a gregarious person and, with his English improving rapidly, he discovered a natural rapport with the customers. Then, in 1933, South Africa came off the gold standard, and almost instantly Jules Street, along with the rest of the country, began to boom.

In their own small way, Max and Fay rode the wave. They increased their range of merchandise and began to carry shoes and clothing as well as dry goods, becoming a general store rather than a grocery store. A few years later, Max bought the bicycle shop next door and the two semidetached houses over the road as well.

With their burgeoning prosperity came a new residence, 18 Gloucester Road. Max and Fay Rubin paid one thousand pounds for a half-acre double stand on the border between working-class Malvern and middle-class Kensington. The family was expanding too: Mickey was born in 1934. Jack followed two years later, in 1936.

Over the next two decades, as Carmen, Mickey and Jack grew up, Max and Fay's grocery business and bicycle shop became well-known landmarks on Jules Street. But vacations were difficult because someone always had to be there to mind the store, forcing Max and Fay to take separate holidays. Years later, when Carmen became engaged to Harry Sher in 1952, Max jumped at the opportunity to bring his son-in-law into the business so as to relieve the pressure on himself and Fay. He offered Harry a salaried position in the bicycle business, which henceforth Harry would run.

CHAPTER 10

Set a Thief to Catch a Thief

I t is Sunday, 11 A.M., a perfect day for repossessions. People will be home, explains Obi. "Also, on a Sunday they will not be expecting you. In this line of business surprise is your best weapon."

It is drizzling softly on and off. Been this way since five in the morning. The sky is one big puddle, emptying itself into thousands of little puddles, filling the depressions in the road and the pavement. Rain splatters on their windscreen. The wipers skid back and forth to little effect, their rubber blades shredded, leaving Obi partially sighted as he turns the nose of his ten-year-old white Nissan bakkie away from Jules Street Furnishers and heads towards the townships.

Veli, twenty-nine, his cousin and business partner of the same age, sits in the passenger seat alongside, dressed in new sneakers with untied laces, pleated tan trousers, and a pullover.

Physically, the two men do not resemble cousins. Whereas Obi's face is smooth and round, with pleasing symmetric features and a winning whiter-than-white smile, Veli is rough looking, with numerous scars lacerating his elongated face. The thick scar down the right side of his forehead is from a knife fight, another on his leg is from jumping a fence and getting cut by barbed wire. The one on his arm is also from a knife, after a brawl in a shebeen, and the scar tissue across his chest is from an acid burn, the work of his girlfriend, he says, after she found out he'd been unfaithful. There are other scars, too—too many, he says, shaking his head, to recall the story behind each one.

Veli slouches across the passenger seat, one eye closed, the other—hooded and bloodshot—half open, a toothpick dangling from the corner of his mouth, and dozes.

"What did Suzette give us today?" asks Obi.

"Heh?" says Veli, observing Obi through his slanted open eye.

"What did Suzette give us?"

Gingerly, Veli picks up the papers on his lap—photocopies of credit agreements and documentation relating to defaulting customers of Jules Street Furnishers—and begins, a little woozily, to read. Last night had been a heavy *dagga*-smoking [cannabis] and beer-drinking session and he is still coming round. "Uh, we have four repos today, in Thokoza, Vosloorus, and two in Soweto."

First stop, Obi decides, will be Thokoza, a township they know especially well because they live there. Veli's papers show that one Rachel Mangope bought her fridge from Jules Street Furnishers for three thousand three hundred and sixty-seven rand, promising to pay two hundred and eighty rand a month, but that she had stopped paying, and that, despite numerous letters requesting an explanation, she had neither replied nor paid a cent for four months.

Obi turns onto a highway flanked by golden mine dumps and guns the engine towards Thokoza, forty-five minutes away to the southeast of Johannesburg. They drive in silence except for the squeak of the ineffectual wipers and the arthritic shudder of the engine.

"Slow down," growls Veli. "Too much vibration. I feel rough."

"I'm not even going fast," says Obi.

"Well it *feels* fast," grumbles Veli.

"I would say plus minus ninety," guesses Obi.

"At least one hundred," says Veli.

"Ninety," insists Obi.

The speedometer—stubbornly stuck on zero—is of no help. Like everything else on the instrument panel, it has long ceased to function. The petrol gauge, which indicates a reassuringly full tank, is not working. Nor is the constantly flashing "petrol-empty" warning light. "Both broken," Obi grins. "We must just guess." Sometimes they guess wrong, he admits. Three weeks ago they were returning from a repossession in Benoni—fridge, stove, and hi-fi on the back—when suddenly, with a lurch, the bakkie stopped. "I had to walk two kilometers to find petrol while Veli watched over the goods. *Aish!*"

The interior of the vehicle—stripped to its bare essentials—looks like a car from a war zone. There is a gaping hole in the dashboard where once a radio-tape player had been, there are no seat belts and no handles to wind down the windows. Instead, whenever Obi or Veli want to raise or lower the window they do so with a spanner stored in the open cubbyhole.

Their stripped-down bakkie is their office. In this respect, they are not dissimilar to their bosses. For, just as Harry and Jack could furnish their office with thick carpets, expensive desks, and elegant furniture—they are, after all, in the business—but instead have only the bare essentials, so Obi and Veli, as former carjackers, could have had their car of choice, but elect instead to drive a barely roadworthy bakkie.

The similarities don't end there, for aspects of their chemistry are pure Harry and Jack. Obi is calm and cool like Jack, Veli is volatile like Harry—and they also use the confines of their "office" to entertain themselves with a constant stream of good-natured, rib-ald invective.

And like Harry and Jack, who have no special talent for the fur-niture business, but who happened to fall into it because life worked out that way, so Obi and Veli's foray into carjacking had nothing to do with a love of cars, or a talent for stealing.

"I wanted to become a lawyer," says Obi. "In high school I was a student leader, chairman of the SRC [Student Representative Coun-cil] and a member of COSAS [Council of South African Students]. I was a leader. I had potential."

"Me, a doctor," says Veli, his tongue lazily manipulating his toothpick.

"There was no money for university after our rubbish apartheid education," says Obi. "We had food on the table, but there were many problems. And then I made this girl pregnant and I had to support her."

"*Aish,* I was having the same problem. I had a child and no job," says Veli.

"We were twenty and looking to make a living. One of our friends came up with this hijacking idea. He said it would give us a regular income. He said he had connections, people who would 'order' cars from us. You steal to order. You just give them your cell number and wait for them to call."

"There are many reasons people become hijackers," adds Veli.

"Others want to impress their friends. Others want to be notorious, to be known as the bad guy. We are not like that. For me, someone's pregnant, she has to leave school, her parents are upset with me. When I became a father, my father said to me, 'Get a job.' I left school before I should have and I tried for two years to get a job. I tried for about ten jobs—but nothing. I was listening to what our friend said about a regular income. That's when I decided to join Obi and become a hijacker."

Until then, neither Obi nor Veli had a criminal record. "You have to put the law to one side and turn to face what you think is the right decision for you," says Obi. "The law was white man's law . . . and we saw that the people who broke it made good money. Everyone could see who the hijackers were. They were the ones driving round Thokoza in fancy cars. We thought—why not us?"

When Obi thinks back on his life as a hijacker, they were, he says, the best days of his life. "When I was taking cars I felt like a hero, like the guys in the car thief movie, *Newjack City*. In the township, when people go to the movies, they cheer for the bad guys. That was us. White people cannot judge me. If I was a white I would not have had to do such things."

The first thing they had to do was get themselves guns. For this, they simply walked into one of the men-only hostels on notorious Kumalo Street in Thokoza, where they bought stolen 9 mm Parabellums for five hundred rand each. Then they walked home and waited for the calls to come.

Their first order—for a Toyota bakkie—came a few days later. But Obi and Veli did not know where to start looking. "We decided

to try an industrial area near the township. There are many companies there, and we thought maybe we can find bakkies," recalls Obi.

They had no car, so they walked. "After a few hours we were lost
and wondering what to do when this guy pulls up alongside and asks
us for directions. We are busy giving him directions when suddenly
we realize he's driving a bakkie! Then we look again and we see: it's a
Toyota! So we pointed a gun at his head. The gentleman—a black
guy—he came out of the car so fast. We took him and drove off and
dropped him off at a deserted cemetery."

"White and black is just the same to us," says Veli.

"He was so scared, man," says Obi.

"But you feel good, you feel nice, 'cos you know you will get that
money," continues Veli. "We took the bakkie to the buyer. He gave
us three thousand five hundred rand in cash, in hundreds and fifties.
It was the most money I had ever held in my hand."

"A new bakkie costs seventy thousand rand to one hundred and
twenty thousand rand. This guy paid us three thousand five hundred
rand, and he sells it for thirty thousand rand. So he makes the big
profit. But we were happy."

About a week later Veli got another order, this time for a Kombi.
It was a different buyer this time, someone who had heard they were
doing hijackings, and that they were fast. This time they borrowed a
car from a friend, drove to the nearest gold mine, and waited outside
the carpark for a Kombi to appear.

"Fortunately," recalls Veli, "we did not have to wait long. The
first Kombi we saw, we followed it and bumped into the back. We
had heard about this method in the township. The driver [also a
black guy] stopped and got out of the car. We pointed our guns. He

was very quiet. We put him in the boot. Obi took the Kombi and I drove our friend's car. Again, we dropped him off at the cemetery and delivered the Kombi."

This time they were paid ten thousand rand. "We felt fantastic. That night it was beer all round at the shebeen. Hansa, Lion Lager, Castle Lager, Black Label—you name it."

"You know I don't drink beer," Obi interrupts.

Veli laughs. "Ya, it was beer all round and two cokes."

"Those cars were company cars and those companies were owned by whites," continues Veli. "Sometimes we stole private cars. Then we felt a little bad. But when you get paid for the car, you forget about that bad feeling."

Over the coming months, Obi and Veli lost track of the number of cars they hijacked. "Maybe it was ten," suggests Veli. "I think it was less than thirty," squints Obi, "Let's say, plus minus twenty."

They were indiscriminate at first, hijacking fellow blacks as well as whites. "You know, I'm not a professor, but I learnt something about human behavior," grins Obi. "They all get scared, whatever their color. Some of them would plead, 'Don't shoot! Don't shoot!' But they all followed our rules, so we never had to shoot."

"Later on we started to target more whites," says Obi. "I remember one day we were driving through the white northern suburbs in Sandton looking for a Citi Golf. We saw it, we overtook, and then, suddenly, we braked in front of her, jumped out, pulled a gun. I remember her face—this young, white, blonde woman, about twenty-five—terrified!" "Ya," laughs Veli, "she was whiter than white."

Obi swings off the highway, the "petrol empty" light flashing, and heads through an industrial area where, Obi says, one of their best customers used to run his scrap yard. "That man is dead now," says Obi. "It was AIDS. He made big money. We were the little guys."

Obi and Veli built a reputation as township untouchables, they say. But gradually, they got drawn into other criminal activities as well, with other partners, and this proved their undoing. One October morning in 1993 Veli and his friend Njiv were holding up a liquor store in Nigel, on the East Rand, when a member of staff surreptitiously hit the panic button and the police arrived, burning rubber. There was a wild shoot-out, with Veli and Njiv pinned behind their car and hopelessly outgunned. "Njiv was shot in the head and killed instantly, and when I saw him lying there in a pool of blood, I surrendered," recalls Veli.

"They held me in the jail at the back of the police station," says Veli. "They stripped me, hit me on my genitals with batons, beat me black and blue."

Mandela might have been released by then, but in the police force, apartheid-style brutality still reigned supreme, and white police did with black prisoners as they pleased. A month later Veli was moved to Heidelberg Prison where he met dozens of other criminals and hijackers.

Soon after Veli was locked up, Obi hijacked a "nearly-new" Kombi for a buyer in the eastern Transvaal. He drove to Nelspruit to deliver the vehicle, a four-hour drive due east of Johannesburg, but when he arrived the buyer didn't have the money. After exchanging angry words, Obi turned round and headed home. "Suddenly I see, in my rearview mirror, a cop on my tail. He's checking the number plate and talking over his two-way radio, and I'm wondering what to do when, out of the blue, he starts shooting at me. He gave no warnings, nothing. Bullets were thumping into the back of the Kombi. I put my foot on the gas, but one of the bullets came in low and hit me in the leg, so I pulled over, screaming in pain. He arrested me and threw me into Boksburg Prison."

Both men witnessed the dawn of the new South Africa from inside the cells of their respective prisons. In 1994, as the country went to the polls, overwhelmingly voting in Nelson Mandela and the African National Congress, and South Africa became a democracy for the first time, Obi and Veli celebrated and impatiently awaited their amnesty. But, though the release of political prisoners was instantaneous, Obi and Veli did not fall into that category, and they languished, awaiting court dates that were interminably postponed.

"We were tried and found guilty, but when they wanted to proceed to sentence, our dockets had mysteriously gone missing," says Obi.

Veli gives a laconic laugh. "Ya, lots of files got lost. Everyone was buying their dockets back from the police. It can be three hundred rand, it can be five hundred rand, depending on what you've done, but with us, the luck is that it just happened. They really *did* just lose our files. One day we were eating jail food, the next we were free men."

They had gone into prison in the old South Africa, and when they emerged it was the new. Now they had the vote, but no job.

"I decided to continue hijacking," says Obi. "It was the one area where I had skill, experience, and a good reputation. People knew me as a cool customer, one of the best. They knew that if they said, 'I want a BMW,' it would be there in two hours." "Ya, we were good together," says Veli. "We were the best. Even the gangsters, they worshipped us."

It was three years later, in 1997, that they decided to go straight.

A combination of parental disapproval and fear of ending up in a body bag convinced them to change their line of business. "My mother told me to stop," says Obi. "She found out what I did and she was shouting that this is the new South Africa, and I don't have to do this, and that I will get myself killed. She was right. I knew from my friends that cops were no longer arresting hijackers, that they were shooting them on sight."

In Veli's case, it was his father, a welder, who tried to turn his son towards an honest calling. He bought Veli a compressor machine, taught him to repair tire punctures, and trained him up as a mechanic. But Veli never took to the job, and in 1999 decided to borrow a car and become a taxi driver instead.

Obi meanwhile had been working in a garage repairing cars for three hundred rand a week. The garage went through a slump, and he was let go, but he had saved enough to buy an old Nissan bakkie. One of his friends came up with the idea of cooking and selling meat on the sidewalk near the factories. They tried it for a while, but struggled to make it pay. Veli also was unhappy with life as a taxi driver. It irked him to work so hard and earn just one thousand rand a month, petty cash compared to the five thousand rand he could get as a hijacker. He toyed with the idea of returning to his life of crime. Then Obi hit on the idea of using his bakkie to deliver furniture to the township. He had heard you could make a living as a transport rider.

Soon after getting started in their new business, they met Suzette Fish at Jules Street Furnishers and asked her for delivery work. She already had enough delivery men, she told them, but she suggested they might try debt collecting and furniture repossessions instead.

Suzette explained company policy—if people bought furniture on credit but failed to pay for more than three months in a row they were sent a letter; and if they still failed to explain themselves, either in writing or in person, the furniture was repossessed. By law, the company should have obtained a prior court order, but with bailiffs too afraid to venture into the townships, court orders were seldom enforced, and so, in practice, it was left to firms to work out their own system. To this end, Jules Street Furnishers, like many other companies selling on credit, exploited a useful legal loophole—called "voluntary repossession"—to pursue recalcitrant debtors.

For Obi and Veli, this would make a hard job even harder. It meant they had to obtain the signature of the defaulting customer before they could remove their goods. It meant that the elusive debtor had to be present when they arrived, and that they would have to use their considerable powers of persuasion to extract the consent of the customer, but without use of force. On top of this, they would only be paid for repossessions that were successful. "Look," Suzette impressed upon them, "you have to be legit."

Obi and Veli were stepping into the shoes of a long line of failed debt collectors. The context was that in the last few years, the bad debts of Jules Street Furnishers had doubled to almost 20 percent of turnover. Nearly one in five customers were buying goods and not paying for them. Although bad debts have always been a problem in the furniture business—as the accountant told Harry and Jack, "between 5 and 10 percent is perfectly normal"—20 percent was beyond the pale.

The first wave of debt defaulters had been the working-class whites who, at the beginning of the nineties, comprised the largest portion of their customer base. When the Group Areas Act was abolished and blacks began to move into the relatively cheap suburban neighborhoods abutting town and Jules Street, most of their white customers had fled to more remote white neighborhoods to the north of Parktown Ridge. The moment these white customers moved elsewhere, they stopped paying what they owed. Most didn't leave a forwarding address; they simply disappeared. These were people who had been loyal customers for decades, and whose parents had shopped at Jules Street Furnishers when they were kids. But when push came to shove—and this hurt Harry and Jack—these customers had reneged on their debts without so much as a telephone call or an explanation.

The second wave of debt defaulters were black and lived in the townships. Some of these were customers genuinely unable to pay, having recently lost their jobs, others bought goods never intending to fulfill their credit contracts in the first place. Whatever the cause of the default, recovering goods from the townships had proved an enormously time-consuming, fruitless, and potentially dangerous exercise. The only solace for Harry and Jack was that all furniture retailers that sold into this market faced the same problems.

Nevertheless, Jules Street Furnishers could not afford to go on losing millions of rands a year. They had to try something.

A year ago, Jack had hired Andries Barnard, an Afrikaner who worked as a bank clerk but who spent his weekends moonlighting as a freelance debt collector. Like Obi and Veli, Andries had been paid for results: two hundred rand a repossession, or 20 percent of debts collected, whichever was the greater. Initially Andries had seemed like an inspired choice. Every month he would present them with the money he had collected. But then one day a customer who received a reminder letter came in and told them that he had already paid Mr.

Barnard. More customers started saying the same thing. When they confronted Barnard, he didn't deny he had taken the money. "I was short. I was just borrowing it. I was going to pay you back . . . Just give me one more chance." Barnard had surprised them, paying back the three thousand rand he owed, and so they had allowed him to continue collecting. For months, all seemed well, but then they started hearing from their customers again. This time, about three thousand eight hundred rand was unaccounted for. "My bakkie broke down and I used the money to repair it," was his new excuse. Because the amount owing was small, Jack and Harry decided it wasn't worth the effort to make a criminal case against him, so they had let him go.

After Barnard came Plank and Marie Koekemoer, a husband-and-wife pairing who were the Laurel and Hardy of the debt-collecting business. They looked and talked tough, but when push came to shove, they had not measured up to the demands of the job.

Coming after this sorry line of crooked and inept debt collectors, Obi and Veli stood out in comparison as tenacious, dedicated, and—despite their past lives as carjackers—well, honest. Although Harry would take just minutes to establish their true credentials, Suzette had no idea she was hiring a couple of ex-hijackers. All she knew was that she had offered them a trial and they had delivered an unusually impressive full house—four out of four—from their first assignment. She paid them eight hundred and eighty rand—two hundred and twenty rand for each successful repossession.

Later Obi tried to make sense of their new line of business: "We are collecting from people who haven't paid their account. We take them as crooks," he told Veli.

Veli chuckled. "It's like, set a crook to catch a crook."

"Ya," said Obi, "but the difference is—now we are the good guys."

CHAPTER 11

About a Fridge

The rain has stopped as Obi drives over a small bridge into Kumalo Street, the main road that bisects Thokoza township. He eases the bakkie past Makatini Bottle Store, Custico Saloon, and Milkway Cash Store, then turns into a narrow lane partially blocked by a vandalized vehicle, idles down another side street, and pulls up outside the address of Rachel Mangope, a twenty-eight-year-old market researcher.

"Beware of the dog!" warns a sign on the unhinged gate. Veli clambers out, yawning and stretching his legs, and watches as Obi pushes open the rickety gate, crosses the mudflat front yard in three strides, and knocks on the door of the tiny box-shaped, tin-roofed structure. Veli follows, clutching the credit agreement, and keeping a roving, bloodshot eye out for the dog.

Obi knocks again, but there is no response. He gently prods at the door, which swings open. "Hello," he says politely, "is Rachel here? We've come about the fridge." "Oh, the fridge," says a woman's voice matter-of-factly from deep within the darkened interior of the dwelling.

Obi and Veli duck under the low doorpost and step into a gloomy kitchen with no light and no windows. In the living room beyond, through a flimsy strip divider plastic curtain, they see an elderly lady reclining on an old sofa, her leg in plaster of paris and resting on a tomato box. She is not Rachel, but Rachel's mother, she tells them, and she beckons them to climb over her leg into the cramped, airless living room where she, Rachel, and Rachel's sister-in-law are sitting, together with six young children who clamber around.

Obi drops down onto the sofa alongside Rachel. "When did you last pay, Mama," he asks.

Rachel—dressed in a mini-skirt with black velvet top and red mules—is calm and articulate. "I bought the fridge from Jules Street Furnishers in November," she explains. "I was supposed to pay two hundred and eighty rand a month, but a few weeks later I lost my job. I told Suzette and she said if I pay two hundred rand a month, it will be okay. I paid two hundred rand in February and another two hundred rand in March. It's only April that I missed."

Obi glances at Veli, who hands him the documentation. "There is no record of your payment in March," he says, passing the papers on to her so she can see for herself. Rachel rummages in her wallet, and pulls out a receipt showing that she did indeed pay in March. "Maybe Suzette made a mistake," Obi says to Veli. "If she hasn't paid for just one month, I don't think we are supposed to repossess."

Obi reaches Suzette on his cell phone. "She's talking crap man," Suzette shouts back emphatically. *"Waar kom sy aan die* two hundred rand a month? [Where does she get the two hundred rand a month?]

That Rachel, *jong*, is seven hundred and eighty rand in arrears. She's supposed to pay two hundred and eighty rand a month. She's giving you *stories.*"

"She says she lost her job in November and you agreed to two hundred rand," says Obi.

"If she lost her job in November, how could she put down a five hundred rand deposit. *Sy lieg, man.* [She lies, man.] Obi, she's taking you by the short and curlies. *Ag,* I can't carry everybody's problems. If they want the goods they got to pay."

Obi listens patiently. "Okay," he says. "What do you want us to do?"

Veli, meanwhile, has begun inspecting the waist-high fridge and is itching to begin emptying it of its contents. Inside are slim pickings: a half-eaten tin of jam, a plastic bottle of cooking oil, and some beetroot and rice in a pot, leftovers from the night before.

"We have no money for food," Rachel tells Veli, apologetically. "Some weeks we eat nothing but *pap.* Sometimes we are going hungry." Prior to being made redundant, she tells him, she was the extended family's main breadwinner. She had been a market researcher earning one thousand rand a month, and she bought the fridge from Jules Street Furnishers because, after comparing prices, they were the cheapest. It was her first purchase from them, but now she has no income, she says, apart from the two hundred rand maintenance she gets from the father of her children, and that two hundred rand goes to Jules Street Furnishers for the fridge, because without it, she says, her children will die.

To illustrate her bona fides, she pulls out a folder of unpaid bills from under the sofa cushion and holds up the latest invoice from Alberton Town Council. It shows that they are twelve thousand five hundred and forty-five rand in arrears for rent, water, refuse, and electricity. "We can't afford to pay *nothing,*" she tells Veli, flicking the invoice angrily with her index finger. "The council say they are sending the sheriff to take away our house. What can I do? I have my matric [school-leaving diploma] and I keep trying for jobs. Last week I phoned yet another market research company who say they will get back to me. Meantime, what must I do? Unemployment here in Thokoza is more than 80 percent. I live in fear. If I see a van coming, I just pray. That is why when you knocked I didn't answer the door. I thought you were the sheriff come to take away our house."

The children squat on the concrete floor and quietly watch TV. It turns out that as many as thirteen people live in this unfeasibly cramped dwelling, comprised of two tiny bedrooms, a living room, and a kitchen, with an outside toilet and a stainless steel bucket for a bath. Rachel's parents sleep in the first bedroom on a sagging thirty-year-old double bed, on which sits a giant yellow teddy bear and a large red comb. Six people squash into the second bedroom: three young children sleep head-to-toe-to-head on a narrow single bed, two teenage children lie head-to-toe on the other single bed, and Rachel's sister squeezes between them on a sponge mattress laid out on the floor. The room is otherwise unfurnished, apart from filthy curtains hanging limply by the window and a rusting Fuchs fridge, with its door ripped off, that is placed between the beds as a bookshelf for the children's school exercise books. The remaining five occupants of the house bed down in the living room, spreading themselves over the sofas and cushions on the floor.

Obi is still on the phone debating with Suzette. "It would have helped if Rachel had phoned to explain," she says, softening now from her initial unyielding response. "I don't want to get ugly with my customers, but I have a job to do."

"I'm with you," says Obi. "What do you want us to do?"

"Okay," says Suzette, "let her pay two hundred rand every month. Let's ride with her a bit and see."

Obi clicks off his cell, and passes on the good news to Rachel. "*Ai*, life in this new South Africa is going from bad to worse," she sighs. "I don't blame Suzette. I know she tries to make a plan. But things are hard, man."

"*Ya*," says Obi, "the new South Africa is same as the old. We blacks are still expected to make a living out of nothing."

"I have no comment on that man, Mbeki," continues Rachel. "I'm not working, my sister is not working; to me he's not working either."

"The only thing he's interested in is AIDS," says Obi.

"It doesn't bring jobs. *Ai*, I don't know what's wrong with him. Maybe he's having AIDS himself."

Back in the bakkie, Veli takes the wheel. It's his turn to drive. "I'm pissed off," Obi says, scowling. "Suzette makes a mistake, we go, spend all that time, get nothing. Do they pay us? Nothing."

"Where to now?" asks Veli, toothpick still dangling from the corner of his mouth.

It's a fifteen-minute drive to the next target, across the relentlessly flat neighboring township of Katlehong, and onto the adjacent township of Vosloorus. There have been improvements in the townships since 1994, says Obi. Roads have been tarred, traffic lights installed, electricity supply provided, and many new houses have been built. "This road we're on now, it's new. These street lights, new too," points Obi, as they pass a lone billboard warning residents about tuberculosis and advertising the services of the Boksburg Health Clinic.

As Veli drives, Obi explains their style of doing business. They use no intimidation, he says, and no longer carry guns. Most of the time, their moral authority is enough to engineer a positive result. "We prefer to repossess from women," adds Veli. "The men can get aggressive. If they resist, we just leave. I don't want to die for a fridge."

Now, arriving in Vosloorus, once again it's a fridge they're after. This time, the front door is locked and bolted, and so Veli strolls round the back, across the mud-slick yard, and knocks at the security grille. "There is the fridge," Veli says to Obi, pointing at a king-size fridge-freezer visible behind the half-open door.

"Hello?" a mellifluous voice ventures from inside, "can I help you gents with something?"

A young woman unlocks the security gate and introduces herself. "I'm Bongi," she says, smiling sweetly. Obi wipes his feet on the mat, but Veli barges right in, making muddy footprints on Bongi's shiny white, Italian tile kitchen floor.

"You must be Rosetta's daughter," says Obi.

Veli nosily opens the fridge to peek inside. It's packed to the brim with Coke, Fanta, Sprite and beer. The owner, Rosetta Seko, runs a *spaze* shop, a township tuckshop selling cold drinks, beer, sweets, chocolates, and bread at a profit to the locals from her house.

Bongi taps her fingers impatiently on the counter and watches Veli with mounting displeasure. She is seventeen years old, slim and pretty, dressed in new trainers, new jeans, and a woolly white sweater. Rosetta is her aunt, not her mother, she corrects Obi.

"Where is Rosetta?" begins Obi.

"She's gone out."

"*Ai!*" says Obi. "*Ai,* that woman! Every time we come, she's out. We have to take her fridge. She has not been paying her account."

Veli eyes Bongi. "Do you have a cigarette for me?" he pipes up.

"You walk into my kitchen, you make the floor dirty, and then you want me to give you a cigarette!"

"Just one," says Veli.

"But I can't," she says, batting her eyelids. "We need the money to pay for the fridge."

Obi flips Veli a one rand coin. Bongi hands him a cigarette and sends him outside to smoke. "Shoo! Shoo! I have asthma and the smoke affects me."

It turns out that Bongi is in her last year of high school. She is certain to go to university next year, she says, where she has already decided she will take her bachelor of commerce degree. She was chosen to attend a school in England in 1997 for one month, she adds, part of an exchange program. "Because I am the cleverest in my school."

"Tell Rosetta to phone Suzette to tell her about her problems," Obi shouts to Bongi as they leave. "We always come here and don't find her. Maybe this is the fourth time. Maybe she is hiding under her bed. Next time we will take the fridge."

Back in the bakkie, Obi has no sympathy for Rosetta. "She's full of shit, that lady. She has expensive rings on her fingers, but she won't pay the five hundred rand that she owes."

"That lady is a *crook*," Veli adds emphatically, cigarette dangling from one corner of his mouth, the toothpick still lodged in the other.

Veli takes the wheel again. It is 12:30 P.M. This time they're headed for Soweto, about forty kilometers to the west. It is raining again. Obi squints through the squeaking wipers. They have been on the road for one and a half hours, and so far they haven't earned a cent. "You can see what drives people to become criminals," Obi reflects. "Ya," says Veli. "Some end up being prostitutes. Just to eat. I don't want to go back to a life of stealing. I don't want to live life by force anymore."

They retrace their route through Katlehong and Thokoza. They pass a sprawling squatter camp called Natal Spruit River, drive through Palm Ridge, a township—Obi explains—"of Indians, coloreds, and blacks," then bypass Eden Park, "a township of coloreds and blacks, but not Indians." Located about twenty-five kilometers to the south of Johannesburg, this is a part of South Africa that few whites ever enter, a poverty-ridden landscape of seamless, depressing low-rise townships with monotonous single-story houses and occasional sparsely-supplied shops. More than a million South Africans live here, but there is no money, no employment, no entertainment, no commercial enterprise.

Turning onto the M7, the highway to Soweto, Veli sails straight through a red traffic light. The bakkie's brakes, he explains without apology, don't work well on wet roads, and so by the time he saw the red light, it was too late to stop. He turns onto the R554, a four-lane main road, and barrels past open fields with high golden grasses swaying in the wind. Obi stares out of the window in quiet contemplation. "One day I want to stop and paint this scene," he says. "Or put it in a poem. I like writing love poems."

Veli grins wickedly. "Why don't you write me a love poem so that I can give it to my *cherrie* . . . A sexy one, heh. None of that soppy shit."

Veli shoots another red light, this time narrowly missing an oncoming vehicle, then cool as you like he cuts across two lanes, turns onto the M68, a six-lane highway, and enters Soweto. He drives through Diepkloof, past the notorious Johannesburg Prison, ironically dubbed "Sun City" by the inmates, and turns into Old Potchefstroom Road. Suddenly the commercial enterprise thickens. There is a strip of fast-food joints, including Nando's and Chicken Licken, and giant, brightly-colored billboards advertising abortions and Aquafresh toothpaste ("kiss bad breath goodbye"). They pass Baragwanath Chris Hani Hospital, roadside hawkers selling rusty exhaust pipes, and the hooting pull-in, pull-out taxi ranks.

"Many of those taxis are hijacked vehicles," remarks Obi.

Veli lets out a one-syllable guffaw. "We have delivered a few ourselves."

Veli veers off towards Orlando, cruises past the Orlando Power Station, and heads for Dobsonville, one of the poorest parts of Soweto. "Not a place you want to get lost at night," remarks Obi.

Again, Veli is reticent to use his breaks, and he skids through a stop sign at the intersection of the Elephant Trading Store, but this time he is spotted by a black policeman in a car hidden behind a tree, who signals that he should pull over. Veli comes to a gravel-crunching halt along the side of the road, leaps out of the bakkie and jogs over to the policeman, who remains seated. A woman walking by with a parcel of shopping balanced on her head turns her neck ever so slightly towards Obi and says, "That policeman is always there. He is asking for money."

Veli comes trotting back to the bakkie like a young pup with a bunch of forms in his hands. A pot-bellied policeman wearing tinted dark glasses saunters behind him. "License?" he says.

Veli rummages through the cubbyhole. "*Shhhit,*" he mumbles. "I left my license at home."

"That is a one-hundred-rand fine," says the policeman, licking the nib of his pen and flicking open his ticket book. "One hundred rand. Plus, there is the fine, maybe another one hundred rand, for driving through a stop sign." He coughs. "Come with me . . ."

Obi whispers something to Veli and slips him two twenty rand notes.

Veli and the policeman retreat to the back of the bakkie to continue their conversation.

"I have some sandwiches for you," offers Veli.

"Thank you, but I am not hungry today," replies the policeman, now beginning to write out the ticket.

"Would this help?" says Veli, extending a carefully folded twenty rand note between his thumb and his forefinger.

"I'll tell you what," says the policeman, "I'll let you off for the stop sign, but I must give you a ticket for the license."

Veli looks glum. "If you have to," he says.

Fifteen minutes later, with a one-hundred-rand fine in his hand, Veli jumps into the passenger seat, grinning sheepishly. As Obi drives off, Veli folds and refolds the fine until he has turned it into a paper fan. Then he pulverizers it into a tiny ball, working it ever deeper into the palm of his hand. Finally, he starts to tear it into minute pieces, which he drops, one by one, out the window. After all the pieces have been scattered on the wind, he digs into his pocket and hands Obi back his twenty-rand note.

"Bad luck," says Obi.

"*Aish!* I won't pay this shit, I gave him a false name."

"My man!" Obi congratulates him. "When they send us the fine, I won't have heard of that guy. I'll tell them that maybe someone was driving a stolen car with our number plate."

"I didn't mind to lie to that guy."

"You have to think fast in the new South Africa."

"Ya," says Veli, "same like the old."

It is 2:15 P.M., nearly three hours into their working day, and so far they are one hundred and twenty rand in the red. It could have been worse. If the policeman had inspected the windscreen, in accordance with correct police procedure, he would have seen that the bakkie, like an astounding two thirds of the cars on the road in South Africa, is uninsured. (A report published by the South African Insurance Association estimates that four million of the six million vehicles on the roads are uninsured. It means that road users stand a 66 percent chance of being hit by someone who is not even covered for third-party damages.)

The bakkie bounces along the potholed roads of Dobsonville as Obi, driving at a crawl, turns left, then right, then left, scanning the curb for a sign that would indicate the name of the street. "Shit, we are completely lost," he says. Veli clicks open his door to ask for directions. "No Veli," reprimands Obi. "Not here, not in this street. Rather pass that map, check it ourselves." Obi's face, normally cool and relaxed, is showing tension.

Finally, they locate the street and the right house and pull up outside. This time it is both a fridge and a stove they are after. The defaulting customer is Pamela Mtwethwa, who the papers show is thirty-three, single, employed for the last five years as a washer, with two dependents, and who is owing Jules Street Furnishers three thousand, five hundred and ninety-six rand and eleven cents on her account. She hasn't paid anything for sixteen months.

Veli knocks on the side door while Obi heads for the outside toilet to relieve himself. "Come in," says a voice from inside.

A minute later Veli is back in the yard. "That woman we want is not here. She is gone to Pretoria," he tells Obi. "That lady says she is her sister."

Obi pulls up his zipper. "Tell her that when her sister returns, we will come to fetch the fridge and the stove."

"The stove is not here anymore," says the sister, emerging into the yard. "It is in for repair." She is followed by a bare-chested young man in his early twenties, dressed only in jeans. He is, he tells them, Pamela Mtwethwa's son.

"Do you know where the stove is?" Veli asks him, speaking firmly.

He nods.

"So, where is it?"

"It is with the fridge."

"And where is that?"

"I know where they were even up until yesterday," he says.

"Come! Let's go fetch them now," says Veli emphatically.

"We rather make an arrangement," says the son. "I could pay some money."

"Your mother hasn't paid for more than a year," says Veli. "When you pay what you owe, you can have the stove back. And the fridge. But for now we need them. Take us to where they repair it."

The son disappears inside the house, reemerging shortly in trainers, dark glasses, and a faded T-shirt. He jumps into the bucket seat, squeezing between Obi and Veli, and starts issuing directions.

"Left," he says. "Right." His name is Cornelius, he tells them, and he's also in the furniture business—working as a cabinet maker—and earning one thousand six hundred rand a month. "My mother was working as a cleaner for a woman in Seventh Avenue, Orange Grove, in Johannesburg, but she lost her job when the woman got old and didn't want to pay for a cleaner no more. It's difficult, since I am the only breadwinner."

They drive for thirty-five minutes in the direction of Braam-Fischerville, deep inside Soweto. Cornelius is taking them on what seems to Obi a convoluted route, away from the built-up residential area towards open veld. The bakkie lurches and slides from side to side on the muddy, crenellated dirt track. Obi is down to driving at ten kilometers per hour, and the thought crosses his mind that Cornelius could be leading them into a trap. He has seen his face, which has many scars. The face of a gangster, thinks Obi. He could be leading them to a house full of gangsters.

Another fifteen minutes go by. The hulking Durban Deep mine dump dominates the horizon to their left, emaciated maize fields run down towards a gully to the right.

"Straight?"

"Ya."

"Straight?"

"Ya."

"Shit," mutters Obi under his breath.

The bakkie slides in the mud. There are houses again, mangy dogs, children wheeling tires and walking barefoot in the streets. "Make a left over there. That one. Number 2708."

There is music blaring from inside the cheaply built breeze-block house. "Let's get the stove and get out of here," Obi says to Veli.

"Oh no, the stove is not *here*," says Cornelius. "There is someone here who can take us to the other someone who knows where the stove is."

Obi is not looking happy. "*Aish!* This is just a wild-goose chase."

Cornelius emerges from the house with a toothless six-year-old girl, his older brother's daughter, called Jessica, he says, who he installs, pigtails swinging, on his lap. "She will direct us from here."

"*Aish!*" exclaims Obi.

Obi drives on in silence. Jessica sucks her thumb, only removing her hand from her mouth to point her pudgy forefinger whenever Obi must turn left or right. After another twenty minutes they pull up outside another breeze-block house. Cornelius disappears inside, this time emerging with a wrinkled old man called George who sports a baseball cap. "This man knows where the sister is staying," says Cornelius.

The five of them clamber into the bakkie—Obi, Veli, Cornelius, Jessica, and George—but not everyone can squeeze inside, so they all tumble out again, and Veli jumps on the back of the pick-up truck where he pulls his jacket tightly around him to protect himself against the rain. "We could have been in Durban by now," he says, shaking his head in disgust.

Dusk descends. The lights at the top of the giant apartheid-built pylons high above the road come on, throwing out their harsh high-voltage glare. Another sliding, lurching, twenty-minute-ride later, Obi pulls up outside a third breeze-block house.

The door is thrown wide open. Inside two women sit on the floor and drink Castle lager and listen to *kwela* music from a tape recorder balanced on a rickety wooden table. A baby gambols on the concrete floor alongside. The TV is switched to the football game with the sound turned low: Orlando Pirates, the league leaders, are playing Cosmos. Framed official photographs of Nelson Mandela and Thabo Mbeki are the only adornments on the wall. Cornelius addresses one of the women in Xhosa, shrugs apologetically, and points to the stove.

Veli immediately positions himself protectively in front of the stove—a rudimentary four-legged electrical oven with four burners on top—and lifts up one side to test its weight. The stove looks well-used. Obi unplugs the stove and opens the hatch to make sure there is no food inside the oven. Then the two of them carry it out and load it onto the back of the bakkie.

The women sit stone-faced and offer no protest. "I'm not cross," says the owner of the house, Josephine Dladla. "I'm just surprised. I didn't know the stove Cornelius gave me is going to be gone"—she snaps her fingers—"just like that." She has a hot plate, she adds, so she doesn't feel desperate.

Veli trots back in, drenched from the rain now coming down in sheets. "Do you have any plastic?" he asks, dripping. "We forgot to bring plastic and we need it to cover the stove from the rain." Josephine roots through a brown cardboard box and pulls out half a dozen supermarket carrier bags. Veli trots back out and secures the plastic bags over the stove with nylon.

A few minutes later Veli is back. "Now for the fridge," he says, beginning to unplug it. "No, this fridge is not from Jules Street Furnishers," says Josephine. "This fridge is not even working. That fridge you want is not here."

"Where is it?"

"In Tembisa."

"Why is it in Tembisa?"

"My sister, she borrowed it."

Veli scratches his head. "Why did you lend her your fridge when yours is not working?"

"I'm not working. I don't have food. I don't need a fridge," she replies.

"I don't believe it," mutters Veli.

"I'm eating mielie meal and porridge. For that I need a stove, not a fridge."

"*Aish!* What's your sister's address? We will go and get it."

"I don't know it exactly," she says. "I can find out tomorrow. I will phone and tell her to take the fridge back to the shop."

Veli trots back to the bakkie to report the bad news to Obi. "I don't believe her," says Obi. He rests his head in his hands, thinking a minute. He looks up. "There is nothing we can do." Veli saunters back into the house and says very firmly to Josephine, "If your sister doesn't bring the fridge back, we are coming back to take *you* to Tembisa to fetch it."

Cornelius hops in the bakkie alongside Obi, George, and Jessica. Veli climbs on the back with the stove in the driving rain.

"Sometimes I feel bad when we take people's stuff," Obi tells Cornelius, "but that woman was a liar." Obi hands Cornelius a voluntary repossession order. "Sign here," he says. Cornelius makes a scribble and hands back the paper.

"I notice your aunt didn't seem too upset about giving up the stove," Obi continues.

"Ya, I told her we had to give the stove back because we were trading it for something better. It's not necessary for them to know my personal business. I don't want my mother to be embarrassed."

"And that business about the stove being in for repairs?"

Cornelius laughs. "Ya, that part was not true." He stares impassively ahead. "*Ai!*" he says. "*Ai,* but my mother will be disappointed. That stove was her asset."

Obi eases the bakkie back over the mud-slick streets whence they came. He drops off George, then Jessica. Veli eagerly jumps back inside the cab, wet and shivering. "*Aish!* I'm cold!" he exclaims, turning up the heater full blast. They pass Dobsonville Prison. "I spent a good few nights in there," says Cornelius. Obi and Veli grin knowingly. As they reach the highway, they drop off Cornelius, giving him the five rand taxi fare it would cost to get home.

"I'm hungry," growls Veli. It's 6:30 P.M. and they haven't eaten all day. Obi pulls up at a garage on the outskirts of Soweto. He puts thirty rand's worth of petrol in the tank and they buy two Power Burgers and chips at Chicken Licken from a woman behind a bullet-proof glass counter. Obi downs a can of Coke, Veli a Creme Soda. They devour their burgers. "Can't match Wimpy," says Obi, wiping his mouth with his hand. Veli burps. Grins. "Excuse me," he says, "it's the Creme Soda speaking."

Two tired men in a bakkie with a stove on the back hurtle back towards Johannesburg. A road sign says the metropolis is thirty-five kilometers away. The petrol dial indicates "full," the petrol warning light flashes "empty," the wipers squeak and skid ineffectually over the windscreen. After deducting the cost of food and petrol, and the taxi for George, and the twenty-rand bribe for the policeman, they will split just one hundred and forty rand for the day's work.

Obi guns the engine, sailing straight through a red traffic light. An oncoming articulated trailer truck driver violently honks his horn.

"*Aish!*" says Veli, sitting bolt upright. "Slow down!"

"I am not going fast," insists Obi. "Plus minus ninety."

CHAPTER 12

Doing Time

What will I say to Sanji? How will I explain what I have done? Jamal Suliman steers his VW Kombi through the bumper-to-bumper rush hour traffic, from the Jeppe police station to his house in Lenasia South, and as he drives, he is overwhelmed by feelings of shame and fear.

He finds Sanji in their bedroom, at the end of their white Italian-tiled hallway, her smooth porcelain-like face crumpled with grief and wet with tears. Immediately he realizes that someone from the shop must have phoned to say that he had been taken to the police station and that he might be late. When Sanji sees him standing at the door, relief bursts from her face like the sun emerging momentarily from behind a bank of dark clouds. Jamal has been steeling himself. But that sudden flash of relief in her eyes, that look of love and trust, is too much to bear. He bursts into tears.

He desperately wants to be held in her embrace, to imbibe her strength, to be told that all will be okay, to feel safe in her arms. But it is too soon for that. First he has to tell her what he has done.

It will be a big shock, he knows. Especially to a woman who prides herself on being morally upstanding. He retreats into the living room, perches on the arm of their solid oak sofa that he bought from Joshua Doore (recently, his tastes have become more upmarket than Jules Street Furnishers) and waits for her to join him. On the mantelpiece are Sanji's religious icons. "Praise be almighty God," they proclaim, "God is great."

Sanji places herself at the far end of the puffed up sofa and waits for Jamal to begin. For forty-five minutes she listens, becoming increasingly flushed, but without uttering a word. "You bloody fool," she screams at him the moment he is finished. "You greedy, stupid, bloody fool. You had a good job. You were earning good money. Now what have you done?"

Jamal wants to comfort her, to apologize, but she pushes him away. "You have disgraced the good name of this family!" She feels a whirlwind of emotions—a mix of deep anger and shame—that her husband has stooped to theft, but also anxiety as to what will happen next. Their two older children are in their twenties and old enough to fend for themselves, but she has a four-year-old daughter to think about. What if Jamal is put in prison? How will they survive without a breadwinner? How could he be so bloody stupid?

Throughout the night Sanji rages at Jamal. Eventually, at around 5 A.M., she falls asleep, exhausted from yelling and crying, her embroidered pillow drenched in tears.

But Jamal cannot sleep. For days he goes without sleep, hardly eating, withdrawing into himself, mooning around the house, not saying much. On the following weekend his brothers and sisters come round to find out what has happened. They, too, are angry with him. "Why did you do it?" they want to know. He has no answer to their questions either. He only has more questions. "How will I pay back what I took? Will Ronny help? Will I go to jail?" He is terrified of prison. Every time he hears a car in the road at night he runs to the window and peers, heart beating wildly, through a corner of the thick drapes, convinced the police have come to pick him up. He tells himself, "Maybe Mr. Sher is right. Maybe I am better off dead."

With growing alarm Sanji watches her husband physically deteriorate. He is already a slight man, weighing just fifty-two kilograms, and as the pounds slip off him, he begins to look unhealthily gaunt. "Don't do anything silly," she says to him. "Things will work out. God is great."

Jamal starts to pray every day. "Please God, have pity on me and give me my job back. I am in your hands. I will never do it again. Only you can save me now." He repeats these words night after night like a mantra.

A few weeks later an envelope arrives with a summons inside instructing Jamal to appear in court. Tremulous with fear at the prospect, he telephones his friend, Detective Inspector Rich Molepo, who confirms that his court date is set for the following month. Molepo recommends a defense lawyer, a white Afrikaner called Fanie du Toit.

When Jamal calls Mr. du Toit, the lawyer tells him his fees will be four thousand rand. Jamal panics at the thought of all that money, but Sanji is resourceful. She sells her jewelry to raise the down payment.

A few days before the case is due to appear Jamal meets his lawyer in town for a private consultation. "I want to change my plea to involve the other manager, Ronny Sher," he tells him. "He was in it with me. I want to say that he was stealing more than I did, and that he led me astray."

Fanie du Toit thinks a minute, doodling on his notepad. "*Ag,* I think you should keep it simple," he says. "Otherwise, the case can go on forever."

"No, that Ronny Sher is even more guilty than me. And I am only willing to pay my half of the sixty thousand rand. I am not prepared to pay for the half stolen by Ronny."

"Look, Mr. Suliman," du Toit says brusquely, "they already have a signed confession from you. But maybe, if you plead guilty, we can get them to settle on thirty thousand rand. And because it is a first offense, I am sure the judge will be lenient and that you won't have to go to jail."

As the February court date for Jeppe Number One Magistrate Court approaches, Jamal is as skittish as a gazelle. And then, all too quickly, he is there, in the dock, his hands writhing like snakes.

"Mr. Suliman," booms the stern but slightly lazy voice of the white magistrate, "do you plead . . ."—he pauses—". . . guilty or not guilty?"

Jamal rises from the flat, cold wooden bench, sweating profusely. "Guilty," he says, barely audibly.

"Can you repeat clearly for the record, Mr. Suliman?" orders the magistrate. His lawyer, who is already standing in position at the defense attorney's podium, says: "We're pleading guilty, your honor. But my client says he stole thirty thousand rand, and not the sixty thousand rand claimed by the prosecution. You will see that my client's confession makes no mention of an amount. He is offering to pay back that thirty thousand rand over one year."

The magistrate stands Jamal Suliman down and calls Jack Rubin to the witness box. "Mr. Rubin, you are saying that sixty thousand rand has been stolen from you. Do you want to pursue that? Or will you accept the offer of thirty thousand rand?"

Earlier, the young public prosecutor, Ms. Seponono Mofokeng, had related to Jack the offer that the defendant was making and had advised Jack to accept the thirty thousand rand together with a guilty plea, rather than a protracted trial that could end up with them getting nothing. A bird in the hand.

"Yes," replies Jack, "I accept."

"You may stand down, Mr. Rubin," says the magistrate. He pauses to allow Jack to return to the gallery. "Because this is your first offense, Mr. Suliman," he continues, "and because there are mitigating circumstances in that I believe you took the money because your wife was sick, I will delay sentencing you. But you must pay the money back as you have agreed, two thousand five hundred rand a month starting the first day of next month. We will meet again in April to see about sentencing."

Jamal feels relief beyond words that he has not had to go to jail. But when he gets home and explains the settlement to Sanji, she is livid. "How can you agree to that?" she shouts. "Two thousand five hundred rand a month is too much. Where can we get it? We don't even have enough for groceries." With no salary coming in, meat has given way to potatoes. They have already fallen four months behind in their rent to the municipality for their house, electricity, water, and refuse. "Maybe my brothers and sisters will help us," says Jamal. "Maybe I can get a job."

Jamal starts looking for work, but everywhere they want a reference. So he phones Jules Street Furnishers in desperation and speaks to Mr. Rubin. "I want to get a job so that I can start to pay you back. Will you write me a reference?"

"You must be joking," says Jack. "What do you want me to say? That you stole thousands of rands from us? Or do you expect me to lie? And what happens then, if you steal from the next employer? What happens then, Jamal? You should have thought about this before you did your crooked schemes."

The beginning of the month comes and goes, but Jamal does not meet the payment. The police do not arrive, but he receives another official manila envelope, this one with a subpoena instructing him to return to court for sentencing in three weeks time. He stuffs the subpoena down the back of his sofa, stops their telephone account, closes down their Edgars department store account, and tells Sanji that he is going to look for a job in Barberton—where her parents live, about two hundred and fifty miles away in the eastern province of Mpumalanga.

Three weeks later, at the appointed time, the magistrate calls the case of Jamal Suliman. Jack Rubin and prosecutor Seponono Mofokeng are in attendance, but neither Jamal nor his lawyer are anywhere to be found. Thirty minutes later, a disheveled Fanie du Toit dashes up the stairs to Jeppe Number One court. The magistrate, who has meanwhile continued with other business, allows Fanie du Toit to belatedly take the stand.

"What do you have to say for yourself?" he demands stiffly.

"Your honor, I respectfully ask to be released from this case. My client has had no contact with me. He has not paid Mr. Rubin as agreed, neither has he paid my legal fees."

After three months of trying and failing to find a job in the eastern Transvaal, Jamal returns home to find there is a warrant out for his arrest. He calls Detective Inspector Rich Molepo, who explains that he is in contempt of court, and that he should come into the police station and make a statement. The very next day Jamal puts on his best outfit—tan pleats, a button-down checked cotton shirt, and a tweed jacket—and hails a township taxi to the Jeppe police station.

This time Molepo shepherds Jamal down into the bowels of the building, past signs that say "Trauma Room" and "Detention Facilities," to the on-site jail and locks him up. "Don't worry, you won't be here long," he reassures him.

Jamal finds himself in a large, spartan holding cell. It has a smooth concrete floor, concrete walls painted gray, and floor-to-ceiling iron bars to the front. In one corner a mat on a raised concrete ledge serves as a bed, and there is an open toilet in the other corner. He squats, knees tucked to his chest in the middle of the room, trying not to touch anything.

Molepo is as good as his word. That afternoon he handcuffs Jamal and leads him through an underground tunnel and up a stairway that leads from the cells directly into the dock of Jeppe Number One court. "Your honor, I was out of town looking for work and did not get the summons until it was too late," Jamal lies. The magistrate postpones the case for two days so that a state lawyer can be assigned to defend Jamal. "What about bail?" asks Jamal. But bail, he discovers is not a possibility once you have shown contempt of court. Instead, he will be temporarily detained in the notorious Sun City Prison in Soweto.

Jamal is bundled into the back of an armored police van with three manacled prisoners whose cases had also been heard that day. One is up for rape, the other armed robbery, the third for murder.

He huddles in the corner of the van, sick with fear. On the drive to Soweto, two of the men grab him by the throat and remove his gold wedding ring, his watch, and the one hundred and twenty rand cash in his pocket. "If you talk we'll kill you," they warn him, with the roar of the engine as cover. Then one man head-butts him in the temple for good measure. Jamal feels a sharp pain crack through his forehead and his eyes well with tears. "I must not cry," he tells himself. "I must not cry."

They arrive at the prison gates at around 5 P.M. For three hours Jamal is processed—they fingerprint him, record his personal details, issue him prison clothes. At 8 P.M. they offer him a quarter of a loaf of stale bread and lock him in a holding cell already occupied by twenty-seven other sleeping inmates. Jamal takes a top bunk, pushes the dirty, itchy blankets to one side, and curls up, petrified, unable to sleep.

Two days later, as scheduled, Jamal is handcuffed and driven in a van back to Jeppe Number One court. Sanji is there, looking pale and they are allowed a quick word in private. "I will be out today," he reassures her. But the magistrate hasn't found a lawyer yet for Jamal. He postpones the case for another six weeks, sending him back to Sun City.

Prison life assumes a dreary routine of its own. Up at 5 A.M. for a cold shower, breakfast at 9 A.M. (porridge with brown bread and a blob of strawberry jam), locked up for the rest of the day until dinner. At mealtimes, Jamal eavesdrops on the conversations of other prisoners. He offers his food to fellow inmates, trading his dinner for their friendship. It works. Thankfully, no one attacks him. Once a week Sanji is allowed to visit. She is alarmed at how much more weight he has lost. "I am trying to raise money to get you out," she tries to reassure him.

Between weekly visits, Jamal has nothing to do but sit around and think about the past. His thoughts turn to Ronny, who is still free, and he imagines him sitting and eating his donuts, having his tea, wiping the crumbs off his handlebar mustache, and greeting the customers. He still can't quite believe that he has managed to fall from being a manager earning four thousand, three hundred rand a month in the old South Africa, to a prisoner in the new. And his thoughts drift back to earlier times, to the youth he would rather forget.

Jamal Suliman was born the middle child of four brothers and four sisters in 1956 in Sophiatown, then a vibrant neighborhood abutting Johannesburg to the northwest. His father, Hassan, was a herbalist, his mother, Meena, a housewife. When he was four, the black and Indian residents of Sophiatown were forcibly removed by the police to make way for a new white suburb called *Triomf* [triumph]. Jamal's family were relocated to military-style barracks on the edge of the Indian location of Lenasia. It would be four more years before the family moved out of the longhouse barracks, built for soldiers not families, and into a two-bedroom rental house on the other side of the railway line.

But Jamal's joy at moving into "a normal house" was tempered by the departure of his father to work in neighboring Swaziland, where he was to achieve a name for himself as one of the herbalist-healers for King Sobuza. In return for his remedies and care, the king of Swaziland gave his father a special plot of land alongside the Komati River. Jamal yearned to be allowed to visit his father. But every month his father would return home for the weekend, bringing his mother money, and every month he would depart without him. As time passed his father seemed to come by less and less, until one weekend his mother discovered that he had been shacking up with another woman. After that, Jamal hardly saw his father at all.

Their father's extended absences and polygamous lifestyle meant that they became one of the poorest Indian families in Lenasia. His mother always managed to put food on the table, even if sometimes it was just bread and butter, but there were months when he went barefoot to school because he had no shoes.

Jamal remembered his childhood as an unhappy time, filled with envy for the other Indian children. Not only were they better dressed, but after school their mothers would buy them lollipops and packets of crisps. "Can I have a lollipop?" he would press his mother. But the reply was always negative. "We have to save the money for your school books," she would scold him. He struggled to comprehend why everyone else got school books *and* lollipops.

In his teens, as he began to venture out of his sepia world in Lenasia, he came into contact with whites, and consequently with the inequalities perpetrated by apartheid. Waiting at a bus stop in town at the end of a long line to board an overcrowded single-decker bus for "non-whites," he watched three empty "white" buses trundle by. Walking into a park, looking for a place to rest and eat his sandwiches, he saw empty benches reserved for "whites only." But worst of all were the insults of young white boys with crew cuts who would stare at him and snarl with derision, "What you looking at, coolie?"

To be insulted by a child half your age was a hard pill to swallow.

"You just have to keep quiet and say nothing," his mother would warn him.

"But why?" he would ask.

"Because it's your word against theirs. They call the police. They arrest you. They *never* take an Indian person's word over a white person."

Jamal emerged into his midteens as a reserved boy with a simmering anger. At school he was above average academically but not sporty. He had small bones and weak muscles, and this made him timid when it came to physical contact pursuits. He was angry at his peers who mocked his frailty. He was angry at his father for never spending time with him and for leaving them in poverty. And he was angry with the apartheid system for the way it broke up families and sent fathers to find work in faraway places. On every front, it seemed to Jamal— physique, color, wealth, family—he had been dealt a bum hand.

The Suliman family finances eventually improved when Jamal's oldest brother left school and got a job as a mechanic. At last there was regular food on the table, and occasionally his brother would even buy him clothes. For the first time he understood that things could get better rather than worse, that they wouldn't be poor for the rest of their lives. One day, he told himself, they would have what other Indians had. One day, when all his brothers and sisters had jobs, they might even live as well as whites.

Jamal left school in standard eight, age sixteen, to work as a manual laborer in a printing company. For the first time in his life he had money in his pocket. On Friday nights he would party with friends. He started dating, though initially he was shy and awkward. At seventeen he had his first sex. At twenty he had his first steady girlfriend.

And at twenty-four he married her. In the meantime, he had left his job in the printing company and secured a better job as a punch operator in a computer company in central Johannesburg. There he came up against the internal politics of the Indian community. The managers were Indians from Natal, and they regarded themselves as superior to the Transvaal Indians. They were rude, insulting him openly if he was even a few minutes late.

He had to swallow enough racism from whites, he reckoned, and so he walked. His cousin fixed him up with another job, this time as a filing clerk earning three hundred and fifty rand a month at an electrical company supplying overhead power lines.

It was the beginning of the eighties, and the black townships near Lenasia were becoming increasingly explosive. There were political marches, police, violence, and, in Lenasia, fear. Rumors circulated in Lenasia that the blacks in Soweto were going to surround them and then kill the men and rape the women and take their houses. Some suspected these rumors were propagated by whites, but they couldn't be sure.

Once Jamal was beaten up by the police for no reason. He was walking home at about 7 P.M. when a police car approached and suddenly someone just leaned out and hit him full tilt in the chest with a sjambok. He fell to the ground as the policemen sped off laughing. Luckily he was just badly bruised. But after that he felt vulnerable, and so he stopped going out after work unless he had to. His best friend, a political activist, would come around and try to get him to come to the township marches and funerals but he preferred to stay in and watch Manchester United play soccer on the TV. He, too, wanted apartheid to end, but he didn't feel brave enough to personally confront the heavily-armed police and the army.

In the meantime, things weren't all bad. He had a wife, a baby, and a new job, too. For by now he was working for Jules Street Furnishers. And he had more money than ever before.

By the time the elections for the new South Africa arrived in 1994, affording him the opportunity to vote for the first time in his life, Jamal Suliman was a thriving family man with a steady job. Of course he wanted apartheid demolished, of course he wanted the ANC to win, but he was also fearful they would win with too big a majority, and he was concerned as to whether a black government would be competent. "Just look at the mess in the rest of Africa," people in Lenasia were saying. And so, "as an insurance policy," he had done what his activist friend considered high treason—he voted for F. W. De Klerk and his "reformed" Nationalist Party.

In many respects the elected ANC government had been a pleasant surprise to Jamal. They had done a good job bringing basic facilities to the townships, he thought, erecting an enormous number of new houses, and they had kept the economy on an impressively steady footing. But he was alarmed by how unemployment had gotten even worse and by how crime had spiraled.

"People just walk into your house and take whatever they want. And maybe they kill you," he had complained to Sanji. So, at night they had locked themselves in. Even though their area in Lenasia South was relatively peaceful, he was still scared. Scared of the criminals who could just walk in and take it all away from you in an instant.

And now, the irony hits him. Here he is, sitting with the very criminals he was so keen to avoid. Sharing a cell with them, breathing the same air as them, taking his tea with them. He has become one of the people he wanted the government to crack down on. Hadn't he told Sanji, "One day we will live like the whites"? Well, it had happened. He had developed a taste for the life! He and Ronny.

But now he is in Sun City prison and where is Ronny? Eating his donuts, that's where, scot-free. Is it because Ronny is white? He feels bitter. But he also blames himself. "I was weak. I should have told Ronny, 'no!' "

CHAPTER 13

Close the Doors, They're Coming Through the Windows

The bright midday sun filters through the slit vertical blinds, making dancing geometrical patterns on the office wall. Jack Rubin looks up from the pile of insurance claim forms he is diligently filling out, his face illuminated by a rectangle of sunlight, a twinkle in his eye. "Sher! Have you heard the one about Abe and Rachel?"

"Oh ya?" replies Harry expectantly, snapping an elastic band around a sheaf of ready-for-posting envelopes and continuing to clear his desk—ticker tape adding machine to the right, wrought-iron punch to the back, in-tray basket to the left—the way he always does when he prepares to go home at 2 P.M. on a Friday afternoon.

"Okay, so Abe is eighty-seven, Rachel is eighty-five, and Rachel dies. So Abe phones up *The Star*. He wants to put in a bereavement notice. 'How much?' he asks the woman in classified. 'It's ten rand a line, sir,' she replies. 'Okay,' says Abe, 'just put in: *Rachel died.*'" (Harry starts to laugh.) "But the woman in classifieds, she is horrified, she says, 'You can't do that, sir!'

" 'I'm a pensioner,' says Abe. 'It's all I can afford.' So the woman, taking pity on Abe, says to him, 'Let me speak to my manager, sir, I'll see what we can do.' Two minutes later she's back. 'Okay, my manager, he wants to help you,' she says. 'He says you can have two lines for the price of one. What do you want to put on the second line?' So Abe thinks a minute. 'Okay,' he says, 'first line: *Rachel died.* Second line: *Toyota for sale.*' " Harry and Jack crack up. Jack's ears turn blood red, tears run down Harry's cheeks, they walk around the office doubled over, puce-faced, shoulders shaking, pissing themselves.

Suddenly Jack's phone is ringing. "Hello, can I speak to Mr. Rubin?" says a well-spoken voice at the end of the line.

"Speaking," replies Jack, still with a wide grin on his face.

"Ah, Mr. Rubin, it is prosecutor Mofokeng here. I am sorry to disturb you, but the trial of Jamal is set for later this afternoon. His family have been making last-minute representations. Would it be possible for you to come through to the court."

"It's kind of late notice, Seponono."

"Yes, I'm sorry about that."

Jack thinks a moment. "But I thought that I am out of the picture now, that since Jamal was in contempt of court, it is simply about the state passing sentence."

"The family want to make you an offer, Mr. Rubin," explains Mofokeng. "Jamal's wife has sold their Kombi and they have five thousand rand to give you as a down payment. They want to pay off the rest over two years. If you accept, it's likely the judge will release Jamal. If not, he'll probably be sent back to prison. But I can't accept or reject an offer on your behalf."

All I need on a Friday afternoon, thinks Jack. More hours

wasted listening to tears and recriminations. "Okay," he says. "What time do you want me?"

It is beginning to sap Jack's spirit, spending so much time dealing with the aftermath of criminal behavior. Too often he seems to be sweeping up broken glass, hiring glaziers, bawling out their security company, filling out police forms, hanging around in court. Not to mention the insurance claim forms cluttering his desk, the result of yet another holdup.

Keeping abreast of the latest scam, reflects Jack, is becoming a full-time occupation.

Take the saga of the fat ladies. Just last week, four fat ladies in colorful, flowing robes had walked into the shop. They looked unusually large, but one doesn't typically comment on the weight of one's customers, and so the sales assistant was happy to let them wander around the shop until she was called upon to render assistance. One of them asked for advice on the vacuum cleaners displayed in the corner and assailed her with a flurry of detailed questions. But as soon as her back was turned the other three began to surreptitiously stuff VCRs under their dresses. The staff only discovered that three VCRs were missing when they came to lock up and return them to their cages at the end of the day.

"Shit, you don't imagine people can hide something as big as that in their bra," Jack commented.

"They came in fat and they left obese," quipped Harry.

Then there was the incident of the customer who paid off his account, only for his friends to steal the money back twenty minutes later. This customer was three months overdue, and he came in accompanied by two friends dressed in sharp suits, saying that he wished to pay off his account. Of course, Suzette was delighted to take his payment, and she had watched as he removed his left shoe, peeled six thousand rand in limp fifty-rand notes from inside his sock, and handed it over. She took the cash, albeit gingerly, and dropped it into the till. Then she wrote him a receipt and the customer duly left the shop, his account settled in full. Fifteen minutes later Suzette noticed that the two men in suits were still in the shop, perusing the goods on display. Thinking nothing of it, she continued with her paperwork.

Suddenly, one of the suits was standing in front of her, a gun dangling casually in his hand, pointing at her chest. "Open the till," he demanded gruffly. So she did. And he reached in and grabbed all the money—which amounted to seven thousand one hundred and fifty rand, including the six thousand rand his friend had just paid. Jack called the police, who visited the recorded address of their customer. But neither the customer nor the cash was ever seen again.

Some of the stings—like the Pie Shop scam—were quite ingenious and clearly the work of professional fraudsters. Three potential customers had come in wanting to buy fifty thousand rand's worth of TVs and hi-fis on credit. They said they were managers of the Pie Shop, a well-known food franchise, and that they were newly moved into the neighborhood. A saleswoman completed their credit application forms, and then, because the amount involved was considerable, referred the credit check to Suzette, who called the telephone number of the Pie Shop that the saleswoman had noted on the credit application form. The voice at the other end of the line confirmed that these three gents were indeed managers of the Pie Shop, and he confirmed their salaries and their dates of employment as well. So Suzette, pleased to have quality clients, passed the credit.

It was only a week later when another prospective customer came in and also claimed that he was a manager of the Pie Shop. Suzette became suspicious and alerted Jack. He looked up the Pie Shop in the phone book, saw about twenty numbers listed, but none corresponded to the number on the credit reference. So he called the Pie Shop head office and inquired whether such a branch with such a number existed. That sick feeling of being had was already starting to well up inside him. "Sorry sir, but none of our branches have that number," confirmed the voice at the end of the line. Next he phoned the number he had been given and when, eventually, somebody answered, he asked, "What place is that?"

"This is The Phone Shop," came the reply. (The Phone Shop is one of those ubiquitous shops that have sprung up across town and where you can walk in off the street and pay to use a phone.) It dawned on Jack that the fraudsters had planted someone there who commandeered a phone, waiting for his call.

Again Jack tried to recover their money by getting the police involved. Again, they came, scribbled a few notes. Then the detective brazenly asked, "Do you want us to try find these men?"

Jack was taken aback. "Er, well, why else would I have called you in?"

"Think about it, sir—false names, false telephone numbers, false references—our chances of catching them are zero."

"That is fifty thousand rand we will never see again!" Jack reported back to Harry.

"Yup. Our contribution to the new South Africa," said Harry.

Harry and Jack tended to make light of their misfortunes, but beneath the veneer of humor, they were struggling to thwart scams that were not only becoming more sophisticated, but also more frequent. With the police undermanned and seemingly unwilling to tackle property crime, they realized they would have to take things into their own hands.

They started by trying to beef up their deterrence. To thwart the holdups in broad daylight, they installed panic buttons under the desks that were wired directly to an armed response security company. To prevent after-hours smash-and-grabs, they fitted shatterproof glass and security gates on rollers that slide away during the day.

The robbers responded by changing their point of entry. Six times that year, in different branches of Jules Street Furnishers, they came in at night through the roof.

It reminded Jack of a song they used to sing on long car journeys when he was a boy:

> *Close the doors, they're coming through the windows,*
> *Close the windows, they're coming through the doors,*
> *Close the doors, they're coming through the ceiling,*
> *Oh my gosh, they're coming through the floors.*

So now they fortified the roofs, rolling out electrified barbed-wire fencing over the top of each branch. This again caused a change in tack, with the thieves once again reverting to armed daylight holdups. Harry and Jack responded by locking all their expensive electronic goods in floor-to-ceiling, walk-in security cages. Each shop began to resemble a zoo—except that instead of a lion cage and a tiger cage, there was a TV cage and a hi-fi cage. Some of the electronic items were chained together so that even if you managed to get inside the cage you still couldn't remove the goods without heavy-duty chain saws. Over a two-year period, they spent fifty thousand rand improving their security. But even this was unable to stop the professional gangs of ram-raiders who plowed straight through the window in maxi-taxis and who set to work with blow-torches and bolt cutters.

And yet, defending themselves against theft from the outside—albeit with limited success—is the simplest part. Much harder to cope with, mentally, is the theft from within by their very own managers who they entrust to run their affairs.

Every business has its *ganovim,* and over the years, they have had their share. Every five years or so a new fraud had been uncovered. But it never used to be a frequent occurrence, and so Harry and Jack had tried to deal with it philosophically. So it was that each trusted manager caught with his hand in the till had become the subject of a rueful little rhyme. So it was that Keith was transformed into Keith the thief . . . Farouk became Farouk the crook . . . Dennis transmogrified into Dennis the menace . . . And Hanif succumbed to Hanif the *ganef.*

> *Keith the thief,*
> *Farouk the crook,*
> *Dennis the menace,*
> *Hanif the ganef.*

Harry's and Jack's children had heard the rhyme so many times, they could recite it by heart. And that was its beauty. It was essentially a very short poem, a very short list. In four lines, it captured the entire history of everything bad that had ever happened to Jules

Street Furnishers. And so, while it served as a sage reminder that not all employees were honest, its message was essentially optimistic: This is what has happened to us; this is *all* that has happened to us.

But in the last five to ten years, Harry and Jack have felt less inclined to turn their misfortune into poetry. There are days when the stealing gets them down.

"Who needs this shit? Maybe it's time to find a buyer for the business," one will occasionally say to the other.

CHAPTER 14

Fifty-Fifty

From the day Jack joined Harry in the business nearly forty years ago, everything has been split exactly down the middle. Their share of the equity, their share of profits, their salaries, their vacation days, their weekly half-days off—everything is fifty-fifty.

But the ultimate barometer of this policy of evenhandedness—and indeed of their progress over the years as a business—is their cars.

In the beginning, Jack and Harry shared a rattling, secondhand Toyota delivery van with dodgy suspension. Every morning, Jack would pick up Harry from his home in Orange Grove and they would bounce in to work together—accompanied by their brown-bag lunches made by their respective wives. The van was used for delivering furniture during the day, and for ferrying the two partners back home at night. On weekends they used their wives' cars, a nippy white Anglia in Jack's case, a beat-up yellow Zephyr in Harry's. These cars had been acquired prior to them joining in partnership and were significant in that they marked a point of departure: It would be decades before the two families would again drive cars that were different.

By the late sixties, on the back of the transistor radio boom, turnover at Jules Street Furnishers had trebled, and Jack and Harry were ready to treat themselves to their first *real* cars. Valiants! Out of the box. Brand new. One each. A shiny white one for Jack, a red one for Harry. For the wives it was modest Ford Cortinas.

But it turned out that the Valiants—ungainly, middle-of-the-range family cars—were unstable at high speeds. When the wind blew on the highway, the car would veer and sway, Jack complained. Not to mention their propensity to guzzle fuel. And so, six years later, this time on the back of the early seventies television boom—TVs only arrived in South Africa in 1973—they were ready to upgrade once again. This time they eyed a stunning new maroon-colored, automatic Jaguar XJ6, complete with six cylinders, two petrol tanks, maple dashboard, and tan leather seats. It was to be their pride and joy. The only problem was, Harry and Jack couldn't afford one luxury car each. They would have to share it, swapping over each fortnight. So while one drove the Jag, the other had to make do with the Valiant. But at the end of that fortnight, like clockwork, come sickness, come torrential rain, they would make the switch.

Their wives, too, began to benefit from the expansion on Jules Street. The company bought each of them a Citroen, cars that looked like giant squatting frogs, but that had magical, hissing, hydraulic suspension systems that caused passersby to stop and stare. It was metallic gold for Julia, olive green for Carmen, leather seats all round.

The early eighties saw the partners progress in tandem once more. The Jag had proved to be a sumptuous drive, but disappointingly temperamental, so in 1981 they broke with a decades-old self-imposed taboo and bought German for the first time: a light green manual Mercedes for Harry, a golden automatic for Jack. And their wives got to swap their clunky, though still exceedingly well-preserved Citroens for sleek new BMW 520s. They had arrived. Not only were they driving exclusive autos, but they—and their wives—could each boast one of their own.

Ten years later, in 1991, Jack and Harry were ready for upgrades once again. By now, though, with their success established, which model they drove had receded somewhat in importance. Besides, they had no ambition to proceed beyond Mercedes. Now the decision as to which car to buy was dictated less by reflections of status and more by personal perceptions of comfort and reliability. This time Jack chose a white automatic Mercedes and Harry a red manual one. Their wives decided to swap their ten-year-old BMWs for Honda 160is. As usual, they paid cash.

And so, this absolute equality continued well into the nineties. Over three decades only the color of their paintwork and the nature of their gear systems distinguished the two men's vehicles from each other. But even this minute display of individuality was grist to their everyday one-upmanship.

"Automatics are for ladies," Harry liked to needle Jack.

"I don't need gears to make me feel like a man," Jack would counter.

Jack Rubin had traveled a long way since the day he arrived in a barely roadworthy jalopy to take his license back in '54. He liked to recount the story.

"Our family car was a seventeen-year-old beat-up Ford that had seen better days," he would begin. "My mother had taken her driving test in it seven times, Carmen had taken her test in it, Mickey, my older brother had taken his—all at the same testing station, all with the same inspector—and now, finally it was my turn. I park and the inspector duly emerges, in his tweed jacket; but instead of climbing in and starting the test, he warily circles the car. I can see that he doesn't look in a good mood. He kicks the number plate, which is already hanging lopsided and loose, he inspects the front lights, both of which are cracked. He doesn't look like he wants to get in, peering inside the cabin with visible disdain. My passenger seat is partially collapsed, permanently set at a forty-five-degree angle, and gray and white stuffing is coming out of the upholstery.

"The inspector eventually climbs in, we go for a drive, and after a while he reprimands me, 'Are you using your rearview mirror?' I look in the rearview mirror, but it's dangling off at an irretrievable angle and all I can see, reflected in it, are my knees. 'Yes,' I say, trying to keep a straight face. And I try to adjust it, but it slips back down again. After twenty minutes of mild harrumphing, the inspector directs me back to the testing ground, where I park brilliantly.

" 'How did I do?' I ask eagerly. He gets out, breathing in short angry bursts like a bellowing bull, dusts the stuffing off his tweed jacket, circles the car once again, gives the number plate—now dangling at an even more obtuse angle—another kick and starts to yell, 'You expect me to sit in a seat like that! I nearly break my back, the stuffing is out, the rearview mirror is not firm.' He is red in the face. 'Now hear me! I don't want to see this car in the testing ground ever again! You hear me? I am going to give you your license on one condition—that there's nobody at home younger than you who is ever going to arrive and take their driver's license. I never want to set eyes on this heap of shit again. Okay?' "

And that was how Jack Rubin got his driver's license.

Jack Rubin—born in 1936, the third child of Max and Fay Rubin—grew up in a house with a hundred fruit trees. It was situated on a half-acre double-stand, and in the garden there were peaches, pears, plums, nectarines, apricots, figs, and mulberry trees, the latter soaring fifty feet into the air and dropping delicious ripe mulberries that stained the yard an inky black. Chickens and bantams ran wild, and there was an outside fridge and a chilly outside toilet. Their home—18 Gloucester Road—straddled the border between Malvern and Kensington, and was conveniently located close to Jack's parents' shop on Jules Street.

But towards the end of the war, when Jack was nine, for reasons Jack was never told and to this day cannot fathom, Max sold the family residence before they had found an adequate replacement. It meant that the family would be split up, and the children accommodated separately until permanent lodging could be found. While Max and Fay moved into a one-bedroom semi that they owned off Jules Street, the three children—Jack, Mickey and Carmen—were temporarily dispatched to Herber House, a double-story boarding house for orphaned and abandoned Jewish children.

"It was confusing," recalls Jack. "One day I was living with my parents, the next they were gone and there was this big fellow who I'd never met looking after me." Herber House was a bleak, impersonal institution and Jack coped by cutting himself off from his immediate surroundings. Although he was to spend six months there, including VE Day, he has blanked out almost his entire stay. One day, without warning, Max and Fay came to fetch him and to take him to what they said would be their new house in Kensington. This house—134 Derby Road—was just down the hill from their old house. But as everyone who lived in Kensington knew, a move "down the hill" was a move up.

Despite this improvement, the Rubins remained poor. They may not have actually *been* poor, Jack could not be sure of that, but they certainly *lived* like they were poor. There was never any money for anything apart from basic survival. In time, reasons emerged why Fay was always scrimping and saving and why there was never anything new in the house. Jack had a new sibling, a young brother who, for some inexplicable reason—perhaps encephalitis, perhaps a fall down a flight of concrete steps that happened at around the same time—had developed brain damage as a young boy. Looking after him had come to absorb all of their parents' energy and most of the family's financial resources. Years later, his brother would be moved to a care home where he would die as a result of eating the foam rubber stuffing from a sofa. But meanwhile, for Jack, this ongoing trauma meant that he grew up with parents who were perpetually preoccupied and that he was left to his own devices.

At Jeppe Boys High, then one of Johannesburg's top government schools, Jack's natural ability saw him excel—both academically and on the sports field—without undue effort. His lean muscular physique made him the second-fastest sprinter in the school; he was a talented footballer, a competent cricketer, and a nimble, gutsy rugby player. He did well enough in the classroom, too, and was popular with his peers. His reputation was of an even-tempered young man with a keen mischievous sense of humor and above all, a cool disposition that never seemed to get flustered.

"Everything in moderation," was Jack's mantra. And that was

Jack to a tee: a person who never ate, drank, exercised, or took risks to excess; a person slow to anger, who saw both sides of an argument. The embodiment of the reasonable man.

If Jack had a weakness, it was that he tended to be a passive bystander when his own interests required him to be proactive. His dream had been to become a doctor, but when his parents said they didn't have the money for medical school, Jack settled—despite grades good enough to apply for scholarships—for the lesser option of becoming a pharmacist. He would earn money as an apprentice by day, and study by night, fueled by the notion that pharmacology was "similar to medicine."

Jack grew to despise pharmacology, with its endless measuring and dispensing of minute quantities of powder. But in the early years, it had the virtue of affording him a measure of liberty, and he and his new wife, Julia, spent a few freewheeling years living in London and exploring Europe, taking temporary jobs in pharmacies to pay their way.

Nevertheless, by the time Jack returned to Johannesburg at the age of twenty-seven, he was keen to pursue something different. And so, when Harry, his brother-in-law, suggested that he buy out Max's half share of the business and come in with him on a fifty-fifty basis, Jack was willing to give it a go.

It was 1964 and Harry was expanding. Nothing spectacular, but by slow and steady growth of 10 percent a year he had built the annual turnover from nine thousand two hundred rand in 1952 to twenty-five thousand, eight hundred rand. Physically, he had doubled the size of the shop by knocking through the wall separating the bicycle shop from the original B. W. Becker grocery shop, and in so doing had created a store large enough to sell bigger-ticket items.

He had begun to diversify out of bicycles, adding gramophones (phonographs) and furniture to his product mix. All this was in addition to a second bicycle shop he had acquired in town, where his younger brother Ronny served as his manager.

Jules Street was changing too. In the fifties, soaring rents in central Johannesburg provoked car dealers to look for cheaper premises, and, whereas the new car dealers decamped to Eloff Street Extension on the edge of town, the used-car dealers, with their lower profit margins, were forced to look further afield. Jules Street—the long, straight arterial between Johannesburg and Germiston—was an ideal choice.

The exodus began in 1960 when a dealer by the name of Manfred Hamburger opened "Honest Fred's" at 168 Jules Street. Within a decade there were 130 used-car dealers on Jules Street, each one more gaudy and brightly colored than the next, the majority of them owned by Afrikaners or Jews. The mix of dealerships varied. There were franchise "late model dealers," who sold "nearly new" cars on credit terms. And there were "cheapie" dealers, who sold "no questions asked" cars strictly for cash. It was mostly the shenanigans of the latter group that generated the stories that have become an integral part of Jules Street lore.

One particularly memorable character was known as "the German." His scheme was to offer "cheapie" cars at knockdown prices, take a 20-percent deposit from the client, and promise to ensure that the car would be given a full roadworthy test before it was made ready for delivery. The buyer would duly hand over the deposit, but when he came to pick up his vehicle he would often be confronted with a car that could barely make it off the lot. If the buyer complained that the car was unfit to drive he would be escorted off the premises by two heavies. Worse, the German would then sue the buyer for the unpaid balance, intimidating him with threatening letters from his team of crooked lawyers. The German is alleged to have stolen hundreds of deposits in this fashion before being exposed in a sting operation by *The Star* newspaper.

It was publicity like this that gave Jules Street its bent reputation and secured its place as the seedy, secondhand car mecca of Johannesburg. But not all the traders on the street enjoyed such lucrative business.

Harry Sher, for one, lagged behind, selling to those who could afford two wheels rather than four. Back in the early sixties there was no such thing as gears or speeds. There was just the standard no-frills "cheap Japanese bike" that he sold for twenty rand, and the "quality British bike," the Raleigh, that he sold for thirty-five rand. In those days most bicycles were fitted with carrier baskets and sold for commercial use. Nurseries used them to deliver plants, pharmacies to deliver prescription drugs, grocers to deliver groceries, and dairies to deliver milk; ice-cream sellers peddled around with freezers full of ice pops. Bikes were also becoming a popular means of transport to get to work. For blacks they were a particularly attractive option, because they allowed them to avoid overcrowded "blacks-only" buses and cramped demarcated sections on trams. Later, bikes also became popular with white high school children, who used them for recreation.

The shop had evolved as the bicycle evolved, but Harry was enterprising and always on the lookout for more profitable lines. His next step was to import wind-up gramophones from the U.K. They came in heavy folding cases with metal fastening clips, accompanied by tiny tins of spare gramophone needles, and on it you could play your 78 rpm shellac records. Later Harry imported valve radios and radiograms (bulky radio-gramophone combos that supplanted the wind-up gramophone), and began stocking sewing machines and furniture as well.

Harry's vision was to create a one-stop shop, fulfilling all his customers' basic consumption needs—other than food and clothing—under one roof. From him they could buy their transport, their sound system, and their furniture. And yet, despite this prescient, ambitious concept, the fortunes of Jules Street Furnishers had advanced in only modest fashion.

It was the invention of the portable transistor radio that would take them onto a new level. Jack could not know it, but he was to join at precisely the time that a revolution in home entertainment was imminent. The portable transistor was already widely available in the west, but when it came to new technology, South Africa was stuck in a time warp ten years behind. The miniaturization of amplification had been made possible by the development of semiconductors, themselves the result of scientific breakthroughs in the earlier part of the twentieth century. This revolution in home entertainment would be sustained by the belated arrival of televisions and VCRs, and Jules Street Furnishers would boom on the back of it.

Initially, though, Jack's biggest challenge was of a personal rather than a business nature. He discovered that he was in partnership with a man who liked to run things his own way and who would treat him as the junior, given half a chance.

"In the early days," recalls Jack, "Harry would chew me out in front of customers. 'Rubin, that's not how it's done! Rubin, how could you be such a bloody idiot!' Rubin this, Rubin that. He thought nothing of shitting on me for something he thought was my fault. I realized that if I was going to stay in business with this bloke, I would have to put him right. So the next time he tried it, I told him, 'Don't ever talk to me that way again. You got anything to say to me, Sher, anything at all, you do it in private.' I wasn't prepared to take shit from him. I was either there on an equal basis or I wasn't there at all."

On a grubby linoleum floor, surrounded by boxes of unpacked transistor radios, wind-up gramophones, stacks of shellac records, and bicycle repair kits, with "black music" blaring from seventeen radios at once, Jack Rubin stood up to Harry Sher and a partnership was born.

For the next four decades, the men would get on remarkably well. Even when things got momentarily tense between them, there was one quality that would define their relationship above all others: trust. Jack and Harry would come to trust each other implicitly and completely. "On that," insists Jack, raising his forefinger without a scintilla of self-doubt, "on *that* you can take poison."

CHAPTER 15

Prosecutor Seponono Mofokeng

Public prosecutor Seponono Mofokeng is a rare thing: a prosecutor with passion. At twenty-eight, she already has a glowing reputation as one of the most respected public prosecutors in the country. This is of some relief to Jack Rubin, but it does not bode well for Jamal Suliman, who, this very Friday afternoon, is being driven in the back of a police van from Sun City Prison to Jeppe Magistrates Court, where Mofokeng will prosecute his case.

Seponono—the name means "tall and beautiful" in Sotho—grew up in Soweto, the youngest of three children. Her mother was a nurse, her father a hotel manager, and her initial impetus to study law came, she says, when her parents divorced. She experienced the venal splitting apart of her family as traumatic, but at the same time she saw that she was not alone, and that many, perhaps even most of her friends' parents' marriages seemed to end in acrimonious separation. She was a child suddenly besieged by a long list of grown-up questions. What happens to love? What causes a couple to divorce? Why are there so many divorces happening in our society? How can the process of divorce be made less painful for all involved? She was driven to comprehend the deeper issues underpinning marriage, and the breakdown of marriage. So it was that Seponono studied hard and proceeded from her township high school to read law at the blacks-only University of the North, situated, as the name suggests in the far-flung northern reaches of the country. Her plan was clear—to become a divorce lawyer in private practice.

While she was a law student a tragic event occurred that altered the direction of her career. Seponono is reluctant to discuss the intimate details of the event, but in brief what happened was this: Her boyfriend of four years, the young man she hoped to marry, was murdered in front of her eyes as he sat beside her behind the wheel of his car. It was apparently a totally random gratuitous act of violence by gangsters neither Seponono nor her boyfriend had ever seen before. One minute they were sitting planning what to do that night, the next there were two men at the window, there was blood everywhere, and her boyfriend was sucking in the last rasping breaths of his life. The killers ran off, but later she was able to identify them in a lineup for the police.

"I was the only witness—without me the case would have collapsed," Seponono recalls. "You would think that people would be relieved to put such cold-blooded killers behind bars, but I came under a lot of pressure to withdraw my evidence. I won't say from whom, but I got threats and so forth."

In her darkest hour Seponono discovered the depth of her resources. Instead of buckling under the crushing burden of her own personal grief and the external pressure to back off, she stubbornly came out, guns blazing. "It helped that I was very . . ." she pauses to emphasize her words, "very . . . angry. I went to court and gave my testimony. But the lawyer defending them, he was a clever one. He tried to cast doubt on my testimony. He pointed out that it was dusk, and that it had all happened so fast, and that I couldn't possibly be sure—beyond a reasonable doubt—that the accused in the dock were the killers. The judge allowed himself to be convinced by his argument, and the killers got off.

"After that I put my interest in divorce law to one side and became exclusively focused on criminal law. I saw my calling as a prosecutor, putting people who have done wrong behind bars."

Prosecutor Mofokeng was so tenacious and became so good at her job that fellow lawyers would remark, "She handles each case as if she will be paid only if she wins." Her forensic cross-examination skills came to the attention of the large private law firms, whose lawyers she was regularly defeating. Soon the job offers were pouring in. Nine private law firms wanted her on their side, and offered starting salaries in the region of one hundred fifty-six thousand rand a year, more than double the seventy-two-thousand-rand pay of a public prosecutor.

"The ninth offer was so tempting financially that I almost accepted it," she admits. "I could see myself buying the Golf that I've always wanted, enjoying some of the fruits of my labor. I even went so far as to discuss it with the magistrate. But then I sat down and thought to myself: If you take this job you will be defending the criminals. It's a fact that the best lawyers go into the business of defending criminals. To them it's just business. To me it's business, too. But it's not *just* business. For me there is also a sense of right and wrong. I have watched the best prosecutors being poached by private law firms. I decided: not me, not yet."

Seponono's position as a public prosecutor affords her a unique perspective on post-apartheid South Africa. She attributes some, but not all, of the soaring crime rate to grinding poverty and rising unemployment—factors that understandably drive some people to crime so that they can feed their families, she says. She sees with her own eyes that 80 percent of the defendants who come before her are black—except in the case of drunken driving, where the racial statistics are strangely reversed. Although the world marveled at South Africa's transition to democracy, there is, she says, a feeling among many in the criminal justice system that the crime wave is the consequence of massive inequality between the haves and the have-nots that the transition to democracy did not resolve. The criminal justice system is left to pick up the pieces but it is woefully ill equipped, both in personnel and resources. Seponono alone prosecutes fifty cases a week, far too many, she says, to thoroughly prepare for.

But not all the criminals she comes across are deprived. It would be nice if it was simply a case of cure unemployment and you cure crime, she says, but the truth is more complex. A township youth culture has evolved in the last twenty-five years that glorifies crime and sets up a parallel economy and lifestyle. Breaking the law, she points out, was seen as honorable in the apartheid years. Now that democracy has arrived, old habits die hard. There are people who could live quite comfortably by honest means, but who make a conscious choice to do otherwise.

The Jamal Suliman case is an all-too-common example, she says. "In my opinion, stealing from your employer is worse than stealing from a stranger, because you are both abusing a position of trust and you are stealing from the hand that feeds you. It undermines the key ingredient of trust that any relationship needs—be it a marriage, a partnership, or an employer-employee relationship—if it is to survive." In Suliman's case, the defendant has stupidly made things worse for himself, she says, by his contempt of court in flouting the earlier repayment order of the court. The question is not one of guilt, which has already been established, she says, but how severely Jamal will get punished.

It matters little to her that the defendant is Indian, and the plaintiffs white. "I don't see color in front of me," she says. "I don't accept excuses of race."

But she is aware, she admits, that others see color all the time, especially whites whose cases she sometimes represents.

"The truth about South Africa is that, deep down, most whites don't regard blacks as intelligent or competent," she says. "So when they see me in action it makes an impression. I can see it dawning on these people that this blackie is not as thick as they had expected. I watch their faces change. I enjoy that. Suddenly their eyes widen and they start talking to me with respect."

CHAPTER 16

The State Versus Jamal Suliman

Public prosecutor Seponono Mofokeng rises from the bench resplendent in layers of black, her prosecutor's robe rippling over her stylish dress-suit. "The state calls Jamal Suliman," she announces coolly. She waits patiently while the court orderly leads the defendant up the concrete stairs from the subterranean holding cells below.

Jamal is led past an armed police officer—whose job is to ensure he does not attempt to escape—and is directed into the dock for the accused, a low wooden bench situated to the rear of the representing attorneys. Jeppe Number One Magistrate Court is a spartan, intimate space not much larger than a squash court. The South African flag provides the only splash of color to whitewashed walls. Turning his head as he enters, Jamal sees his extended family sitting in the gallery on the tiers of wooden benches rising up behind him: Sanji, his mother, his grandmother, his sisters, his brothers.

On the far side, sitting isolated and on his own, is a sober-looking Jack Rubin.

"Prosecutor Mofokeng, please proceed," says the magistrate, from his seat on the raised dais up front.

"Your worship, this matter is ready for trial. The witnesses are all present. The state is ready to proceed."

Mofokeng reads the charges, then runs through each piece of evidence in turn. She has in her possession, she says, a three-page, typed affidavit, signed under oath, from the complainant, Mr. Jack Rubin. She also has in her possession a two-page, typed affidavit, signed under oath, from Jamal Suliman's immediate line manager, Mr. Ronny Sher. And finally, she has a handwritten confession from Jamal Suliman. She presents copies of the affidavits to the magistrate and reads out each one in turn.

Watching Seponono in action, Jack can't help but feel impressed with the fluency and thoroughness of her presentation.

When she gets to Ronny Sher's affidavit, she reads: "I, Ronny Sher, state under oath in English that on the day in question, Mr. J. Suliman called me and told me that he wished to discuss something in private with me regarding the missing stock items. He then informed me that the missing stock items were sold by him, and that he kept the proceeds of the respective sales. He also told me that he got into great financial difficulties, that he had to pay out a lot of medical bills that he had incurred during the illness of his wife. He also told me that he had intentions of paying the money back once he had received loans from certain family members. He admitted to me that he had sold the missing stock and had kept the monies. I then phoned Mr. J. Rubin at our main office and told him that he should come down, as we had a big problem on our hands. Mr. J. Suliman told me he was very sorry for what he had done."

Jamal smarts and shakes his head in disgust as he listens to Ronny's sworn statement.

The magistrate allows Mofokeng to present the body of evidence without interrupting, and then calls Jamal Suliman to the stand to hear from him directly. "I see from the previous court order that you were instructed to pay two thousand five hundred rand a month. Why did you not pay?" he says tartly.

"Your worship," pleads Jamal, "I had no job and no money."

"But why didn't you come to court and explain this when you were supposed to?"

"Your worship . . ." Jamal mumbles. He stands silent, looking gaunt and defeated, with nothing to offer in his defense.

Mofokeng calls Jack Rubin to the witness box. "I believe that Mr. Suliman's family have offered you a settlement," the magistrate says. "Are you prepared to accept the new offer?"

Jack looks over at Jamal sitting in the dock. For a moment, superimposed on his rakish face, he sees the cast of characters who have stolen from him and Harry: Keith the thief, Farouk the crook, Dennis the menace, Hanif the ganef, oily Mel Vos . . . All those people got away, never facing charges, never making recompense. Jack is overwhelmed by a desire to make Jamal pay for what he did, for what all of them did. He is sick and tired of wasting his time with promises to pay that aren't worth the paper they're written on. You just get to a point where you've had enough. Send the thieving bastard to prison where he belongs.

The court is silent as Jack's gaze lingers, and then moves on to the family members anxiously watching in the gallery. Earlier, before the court proceedings began, they had come up to him, each one in

turn—Jamal's wife, his mother, his granny, his sisters, his brothers—
to apologize for Jamal's behavior. It had moved him. They had
shown genuine remorse, he felt, genuine appreciation of the fact that
Jamal had done wrong. Besides, he knew that Jamal had children.
He had no wish to deprive them of their father by sending him to
prison.

"Yes," Jack announces, "I will accept the offer."

The magistrate asks Jack to stand down and recalls Jamal for
sentencing. "In the matter of the state versus Jamal Suliman," he
says, "I am sentencing the accused, Jamal Suliman, to three years
imprisonment"—there are audible gasps from the gallery—"suspended for five years, on the following conditions. One, that the
accused is not convicted of theft or attempted theft during the
period of suspension and for which offense direct imprisonment is
imposed without the option of a fine. Two, that the accused pays the
sum of five thousand rand today to the complainant, Mr. Jack Rubin
of Jules Street Furnishers. And three, further that he pays Jules Street
Furnishers the sum of one thousand rand on or before the first working day of each month until the balance of twenty-five thousand
rand is paid in full."

The magistrate looks up. "It is my opinion that you are a lucky
man, Jamal Suliman. Mr. Rubin has agreed to allow you to pay back
one thousand rand a month over two years. By rights, there should
be an interest factor, but I am going to waive that because it makes
things too complicated and because, considering that you don't have
a job, the burden is probably quite enough already. But I want to ask
you, Jamal Suliman, how do you propose to pay back this money?"

"I will get a job," says Jamal, a smile of relief appearing on his
lips for the first time.

"With whom, may I ask?"

"I am hoping to get a job with one of my relatives, your worship."

"As long as you understand, if you don't pay the installments by the first day of every month, you will be rearrested, Mr. Suliman. You will serve your time . . . Good luck, Mr. Suliman. I hope I do not see you here again. Court dismissed."

Jack watches as Jamal is released from custody into the arms of his family. He flings his arms around each one in turn—his wife, his mother, his granny, his sisters, his brothers. Then, one at a time, Jack watches as each of the relatives make their way over to him. They shake his hand and thank him profusely. "Thank you, Mr. Rubin. Thank you for being so kind and so understanding."

Finally, he looks up to see Jamal standing before him. "Thank you, Mr. Rubin," he says, the tears welling up in his eyes, "thank you for giving me back my freedom."

Jack's ears redden at the unexpected show of emotion. "I was looking at your wife, Jamal. I was thinking of your child. I didn't want you to go back to jail."

"I want to live an honest life now, Mr. Rubin. Thank you for helping me. I will never forget you."

CHAPTER 17

The Men in the Rates
and Electricity Department

Jack Rubin is feeling good. The successful outcome to the Jamal Suliman case has renewed his faith in the system. For all its faults, the new South Africa works, he remarks to himself. Detective Molepo had done his job, the magistrate had fulfilled his, and prosecutor Mofokeng, hell, she had been terrific. All around, a good result.

At a macro-economic level, too, there is positive news. The papers report that inflation, measured by the consumer price index, is down to 6 percent, its lowest level for thirty years, and that the all-important prime borrowing rate has been cut to 14 percent. The government has built up sixty billion rand in reserves and has a healthy balance of payments. Whichever way you cut it, these are dramatic improvements on the almost bankrupt economy of the late apartheid years—when inflation was 15 percent and interest rates soared to 25 percent.

"Yaaaa," muses Jack to Harry, scanning the *Citizen* beneath his tea and biscuits, "we are no longer pariahs. The world trades with us, plays sport with us. We are coming back."

"Ya, exports are strong. I'm telling you, Rubin, we are due a boom. We are due a boom. I can feel it in my water."

"Could happen, Sher. Could happen. I heard an economist on the radio. He said we are on the threshold of a recovery. Strong exports, low inflation, low interest rates, stable fiscal policy, all that. We are coming back."

"Ya, ya, but remember, Rubin—you heard it first from *me.*"

Of course, it is not all roses. A file of correspondence with the Rates and Electricity Department—currently sitting in Jack's in-tray—is testimony to the fact that the legacy of chronic inefficiency that was the hallmark of municipal government during the apartheid years still endures.

The saga had begun nearly a year earlier when Jack had become aware that the water account mailed to them by the Rates and Electricity Department of the Greater Johannesburg Eastern Metropolitan Local Council had been skyrocketing in recent months. He couldn't understand why, given that they hardly used any water at all on the premises. They only had a kitchen sink and a toilet in the back. That was it. He checked to ensure that there was no leak and that the meter reading had been accurately taken. And that was when he discovered that the identity number of the water meter on their bill did not correspond to the identity number of the water meter on their premises.

Ah, he thought, problem solved. They have sent us the wrong bill. He phoned the Rates and Electricity Department to report the problem, where a supervisor by the name of Mrs. Roux responded to his complaint, and said she'd send an inspector around to have a look. A few days later, the inspector arrived and confirmed that Jack was correct. He ascertained that the water meter that Jules Street Furnishers had been charged for belonged instead to one of the small privately owned houses that abutted the rear of their premises, but without visiting each one, he couldn't pinpoint precisely which.

Jack meanwhile, had been reexamining past water bills and had worked out that they had been paying somebody else's account for well over three years. According to his calculations, they had been overcharged fifteen thousand rand. And so, following the inspector's visit, Jack phoned Mrs. Roux to claim back the fifteen thousand rand they had been falsely charged.

"I'm sorry, sir," she said, "but we cannot refund the money until we find out who should have paid for the water in the first place."

Jack was incredulous. "But that has nothing to do with us," he spluttered. "We are simply asking for the account to be corrected and for the amount we have been wrongly charged to be returned to us. Fifteen thousand rand is not small potatoes, you know."

"Yes, sir, I understand, sir, I'll look into it, sir," she said.

One month went by. Then another. Jack was growing impatient. He started to phone Mrs. Roux, but her phone just rang. He would hold on five, ten minutes. Eventually someone would pick up the phone. "Hello, can I speak to Mrs. Roux," he would ask. They would put him through. Once again the phone at the extension just rang. And this time nobody would pick up at all. Eventually Jack would hang up and dial the first number again. After an extended wait the operator would put him through to an answer machine where he could leave a message for Mrs. Roux. She never did return his calls.

With mounting frustration. Harry watched Jack getting nowhere. "I'm telling you, Rubin, the only way you're going to sort this out is if you go there for yourself. You've got to speak to the head of the department in person."

Jack was resistant at first, but after four months of trying over the phone, he drove to the high-rise offices of the Rates and Electricity Department in Braamfontein, just north of the city center. He had no appointment. In reception, a sign said: "No unauthorized personnel beyond this point." Jack walked right on by. He kept going, unchallenged, past the security guards at the base of the elevators, up the elevator, through the maze of cubicles, asked someone who the head of the department was—"a white guy called Mr. De Vaal," one of the staff advised him—and walked into his office and sat down in front of him.

As soon as Mr. De Vaal had overcome his surprise at the unexpected intrusion, he was sympathetic to Jack's case. "Mrs. Roux has not been back to you because she is on a training course," he said. "Rest assured, Mr. Rubin, I will look into this matter myself. I will try and sort it out for you. You have my word."

Six weeks went by and Jack heard nothing. So he started phoning again. Same story: He couldn't get through. And when he did he got an answer machine. When he left messages no one returned his calls.

So he went to visit Mr. De Vaal again. This time he took with him a typed, one-page letter that explained the whole story. Again, he walked straight through the security check and into the office of

Mr. De Vaal and reintroduced himself. Mr. De Vaal could only vaguely remember Jack, he said, and he was even vaguer about the details of the query. Jack patiently showed him the letter he had typed up that concluded with the line: "We are now at the end of our tether and request immediate attention." Mr. De Vaal led Jack to the nearby office of another supervisor, a Mr. Lawrence. Jack showed him the letter and was asked to repeat the whole story. "Okay," said Mr. Lawrence, listening attentively, "I will credit your account and phone you to confirm on Friday."

Friday came and went. No call. A month later Jack called the department again. "Sorry sir, but Mr. Lawrence is no longer with us," the voice said. "He left a few weeks ago. Is there anyone else who can help?"

By now Jack is ready to hand the case over to lawyers, which means further expense, and possibly the courts, a course of action he does not relish. It takes the successful outcome of the Jamal trial to burnish his natural optimism. He decides to try one more time.

So back Jack goes. Once again, he barges into Mr. De Vaal's office. But this time he's not taking shit. This time his stride is firm and his ears are flaming. "Right, Mr. De Vaal, it's me, Jack Rubin. Remember me? Good. That's an improvement. I want to tell you, Mr. De Vaal, I've had enough of your broken promises. I want to know *who's* sorting this mess with our water account, and I want to know *now*."

Mr. De Vaal is seemingly unperturbed by the force of Jack's opening statement. "It was bad luck that Mr. Lawrence left," he says laconically. "I have another supervisor, though. He's recently joined us. Let me take you through. I am sure he can help you out."

Supervisor number three—as Jack calls him—asks to be put in the picture and, yet again, Jack obliges, recounting the whole sorry saga from beginning to end and showing him his by now well-folded summary letter.

"Yesss," responds the supervisor, scratching his chin as he reads, "I can see that what you say is correct." He looks up. "But I can't give you credit for fifteen thousand rand."

"Why not?" challenges Jack.

"The accountants will ask all kinds of questions."

"But you are the supervisor," says Jack. "Surely your job is to make a determination on the matter and then pass explanation to the accountants. I don't understand your logic."

"Yesss . . . I hear what you say," says the supervisor. "I will speak to the accountants and get back to you."

"No way," says Jack, rising to his feet. "No way. Look, I'm sorry, but I can't come back here again. I just can't."

"It will only take a week or two, sir."

"A week or two?" explodes Jack. "Listen, I have been messed around for a year on this. Your department owes us fifteen thousand rand and they are refusing to credit us. This is theft, sir. Theft. You know you owe us the money, you even admit it, what do I have to do to get you to pay it? I'm not leaving your office until you fix it up. I will sit here all day if necessary, here, on this chair in front of your desk. You have a choice: Either you sort it out now, or you have me in your office, in your face, the rest of the day."

Supervisor number three rises from his chair. "Let me see what I can do," he says.

Fifteen minutes later he's back. "It's done," he says smiling. "A credit for fifteen thousand rand has been passed and will appear on your next statement."

"Music to my ears," says Jack, grinning. "Music to my ears." Jack is about to leave when a thought crosses his mind: What if, despite the supervisor's claim, a credit is not passed? What if it's all a bluff to get him out of the office? "One more thing, sir," he says. "Whenever I call, I can never get through to anyone in your department. Just in case we need to speak again, sir, just in case, I have one last request—your personal cell phone number. That way, I know that when I call there will be a human being who knows what I'm talking about at the other end of the line."

The supervisor smiles self-consciously, roots around for a pen, and writes it down for Jack. As he hands it over he straightens up, clears his throat, and says: "Now that I have helped you, Mr. Rubin, eh, maybe you can help me." Jack stops. "My wife, she works there in Kempton Park, and she has to commute every day from our home in Johannesburg. It's a long journey and I'd prefer her to work closer by. I was wondering: Do you have a vacancy for her in your shop?"

"Look," says Jack, "we have nothing at present. But I can certainly keep her in mind."

A week later, almost a year to the day after the dispute first came to Jack's notice, they receive a statement from the Rates and Electricity Department showing that their water account has been credited, as promised, with fifteen thousand rand.

"So, what do you think, Mr. Pink?" Jack says triumphantly to Harry, brandishing the water account like a winning lottery ticket.

Harry looks up from punching numbers—*clack, clack, clack*—into his adding machine. "Finally you came through, Rubin. Didn't I tell you, didn't I say that if you wanted something to happen, you had to get your arse over there?"

Jack grins. "Is that the best you can do, Sher? Come on, Sher, break down. Give a credit. Give a 'well done.' Don't make me pull it out of you, Sher."

CHAPTER 18

The Mystery of the Empty Cash-Drop Box

Three weeks after Jamal makes his first payment in accordance with the court judgment, Harry Sher receives an urgent call from their bank manager at First National Bank.

"Mr. Sher," says the bank manager, his Afrikaans accent heavy with earnestness, "a cash-drop box has arrived at our bank from your downtown branch with a deposit slip that says there should be eleven thousand one hundred and eight rand in the box, but I have to inform you that the box is empty."

"What do you mean it's empty?" says Harry.

"I mean there is no money in it."

"Are you telling me that eleven grand is missing?"

"It appears so, Mr. Sher. If you would like to come down to the bank, we record the opening of all drop boxes on video. I suggest you come and view the footage for yourself."

Harry slumps in his chair. For the last seven years, ever since Jack was attacked, they have used Maximum Security Services to do their banking, paying ten thousand rand a month for the service.

With only two people having access to the cash in the drop box—the branch manager and the Maximum Security Services operative—it's a method that is supposed to be foolproof.

The system works as follows: A two-way safe is built into the shop wall. At the end of the trading day the manager empties the cash takings, together with a deposit slip, into a prenumbered plastic bag. The manager places the bag into a slot on top of the drop safe and pushes a lever, whereupon the bag falls with a *clunk* into the steel container inside the safe. The lever is pulled back to its original position, sealing the steel container, and that, theoretically, is the end of their involvement with the cash deposit. Later, usually the next morning, an armed Maximum Security Services operative arrives and opens the safe door from the street side. He extracts the container, which upon removal, is automatically locked. He then slides a new empty container into the safe, ready for the next cash drop, slams the safe door shut, locks it, and delivers the locked drop box to the bank.

This system operates routinely every day, and is identical to that employed by thousands of other companies that use Maximum Security Services throughout the country.

If eleven grand has disappeared into thin air, Harry's mind races . . . either the Maximum Security Services employee must have stolen it, or Ronny, his brother, the branch manager, must be responsible.

There was a time when Harry would never have doubted Ronny. But too much water has passed under the bridge for him to feel that way anymore.

————

Ronny Sher is a man of intriguing contradictions. On first meeting him, he comes across as a straight-up model citizen. At various times in his life, he has been a blood donor, a volunteer firefighter, and the secretary of his local tennis club. On the one hand, Ronny Sher is a civic-minded, salt-of-the-earth guy, the kind of caring, honest person you would be happy to leave your dog with when you go on vacation.

But on the other, his ponderous way of speaking can make him appear a touch dim and he sometimes gives the impression he has a large chip on his shoulder.

In school, Ronny had failed to distinguish himself, matriculating from high school with average grades. Although his aim was to become a stockbroker, instead he went to work for his older brother Harry.

At first Harry was pleased to have Ronny on board. He needed someone he could trust to run his newly opened downtown branch—and who better than family? Initially, Ronny was happy to be employed by his brother, but over the years, and as he grew in confidence, he began to harbor the belief that one day he would become Harry's partner. It was a bitter pill to swallow therefore, when nine years later, Jack Rubin, Harry's brother-in-law, who was the same age as Ronny, joined the business as a partner on an equal footing with Harry.

Ronny was not privy to the details of this business arrangement, which saw Jack buy his father's half share for a consideration amounting to 50 percent of the value of stock and fixtures, plus goodwill. Jack's partnership had nothing to do, in fact, with Ronny's status and everything to do with Max's half share in the business. But all Ronny knew was that his brother was now partners with someone else, and that he, who had worked there longer, was out in the cold.

The truth is that Harry never intended to offer Ronny a partnership. To Harry, Ronny did not have what it takes—being neither intelligent enough nor sufficiently socially adept. On a day-to-day basis, Harry tended to be brusque with Ronny, shouting at him when he fell short of expectations. Ronny appeared to take these doses of humiliation without complaint. He timidly apologized for his mistakes and for the things he did that caused his brother displeasure. He never challenged Harry. He never said, "How dare you talk to me that way?" But beneath the surface, a toxic brew—bred of resentment towards Harry and envy towards Jack—was simmering.

Harry and Jack were oblivious to this. "I was simply the boss and he was my young brother," recalls Harry. "I never saw him as an equal. Our families hardly ever socialized together. But I trusted him absolutely. He was my brother. I always saw him as an honest good guy. Not too bright, but honest."

"My relationship with Ronny was solid," says Jack. "We were never big buddies. Harry and I were more buddies, playing golf on weekends, and our families were close. But did I trust Ronny? Absolutely. I trusted him to the point that I never checked up on him."

Neither Harry nor Jack detected a double standard being applied. Ronny was trusted as family, but he wasn't treated with the warm embrace one offers family. By 1985 Ronny had put in thirty years of loyal service to Jules Street Furnishers. In that time the downtown branch that he managed had become the largest and most profitable of all their branches. Harry and Jack rewarded Ronny by giving him a one-third share of the equity in the downtown branch, elevating him above employee status in the shop that he managed. And when they bought the building from the landlord, thereby doubling the size of the shop, they gifted Ronny a one-third share of the property as well. Ronny was now a one-third partner in the branch he managed, and he enjoyed one-third of the profits he generated, despite never putting any capital of his own into the business. But becoming a partner in the overall group was never up for discussion. From that he was wholly excluded, as well as from the strategic group decision-making.

Financially, however, Ronny was doing nicely. He earned a good salary, twenty thousand rand a month, and he lived in one of the wealthiest northern suburbs in a five-bedroom house with air-conditioning and a swimming pool, the former being a feature of only the most luxurious Johannesburg homes.

In 1986, as the townships exploded and the Nationalist government declared a state of emergency, Jules Street Furnishers found itself embroiled in an emergency of its own. Harry first got a whiff of it when he sat down to prepare the end-of-year branch accounts, and the figures didn't add up. There was a big hole in the trial balance. Something was amiss, so Jack went in and—since these were in the days before their debtors were computerized—manually added the cash receipts for the year on his handheld calculator. When he was done, he retrieved the deposit slips for the year, added them up, and compared the two totals. The discrepancy between what the books said they had sold for cash and the amount actually banked was huge. Cash takings exceeded cash deposits by one hundred and fifty-four thousand rand. That was 20 percent of their entire branch turnover!

At first Harry couldn't bring himself to believe that his brother had been stealing from them. "A brother doesn't steal from a brother," he told Jack. They decided to call in their accountants to provide independent verification.

A fortnight later, the auditors were ready to issue their report. "You are looking at major fraud," they told Harry and Jack. Reluctantly, Harry and Jack summoned Ronny for an after-hours showdown at Harry's house. Ronny arrived accompanied by his wife, Louise, his briefcase in hand. The atmosphere was tense. When everyone was seated Harry began.

"Do you know why we have called you here, Ronny?" he asked.

"No," replied Ronny, his face deadpan.

"We have called you here," Harry spoke slowly, deliberately enunciating each word, "because our auditors have found a one-hundred-and-fifty-four-thousand-rand hole in the downtown branch accounts." He handed Ronny a copy of the auditor's report. "Can you explain this, Ronny?"

Ronny did not blink. He looked straight through Harry as if he wasn't there. But Louise, who is a bookkeeper, took the report and began to scrutinize it furiously. Within seconds, her schooled eye told her that there was indeed a hole in the accounts. She began to shake her head. "This is bad," she said, her eyes darting from Ronny to Harry. "This is bad. I can't understand this at all . . ."

"You're damn right this is bad," sneered Harry, bristling. Harry's method of interrogation was not unlike the way he used to fight in the amateurs. Soften them up with a few jabs, see how they respond, then move in for the kill. "Unless you can explain to us, Ronny, what's happened to the missing one hundred and fifty-four thousand rand, not only are we going to have to fire you, but we are going to call the police and have you arrested." Harry paused and spun round, his face just inches from Ronny's. A corrosive blast issued from his lips. "Is that what you want, Ronny? Is that what you want us to do?"

Suddenly Ronny's face, which had appeared so stiff yet so composed, began to crumble. His shoulders sagged, his body caved in at the waist and he started sobbing uncontrollably, tears running down his red cheeks. "I am sorry," he said between long, deep snivels. "I am sorry. I swear, Harry, I swear it will never happen again." Harry was still circling with intent, glaring at his younger brother with total disdain. Ronny kept on repeating the phrase: "Please don't fire me. Please don't call the police."

Jack, who until then had let Harry do the talking, asked Ronny to tell them how he had done it. When Ronny had recovered himself somewhat, he started to explain. "If I was meant to bank five thousand rand, I'd bank four thousand and pocket the difference. But I didn't," he paused, his blue eyes wide with fright, "it couldn't have been as much as one hundred and fifty-four thousand rand. I don't believe I took as much as one hundred and fifty-four thousand rand."

"How do you know whether you took fifty-four thousand rand or one hundred and fifty-four thousand rand?" shouted Harry. "You fucking crook! You just took, you just grabbed, you just stole. You didn't stop to count, did you?"

Next thing Ronny was on his feet, briefcase in hand, and with a detached, almost surreal calm had excused himself to go to the bathroom. Louise shouted, "Harry! He's got a gun in his briefcase! Stop him! Quick!" Harry sprinted after Ronny and tackled him from behind. Ronny, Harry, the briefcase and the gun all went flying. Harry dusted himself off and yanked Ronny to his feet. "Whatever you have done," he said, speaking tersely and out of breath, "it is not worth taking your life. It is not worth leaving your wife and your children without financial support. Now get back into my living room and let's talk about where we go from here."

Just in time, Carmen emerged from the kitchen with a tray of tea and biscuits to calm everyone's nerves. After conferring momentarily with Jack in the second living room, Harry told Ronny, "Okay, we are prepared to give you another chance. *But*, we're taking away your share of the equity in the company and the property. You will have to sign it over. From now on, you will just be an employee like everybody else."

Ronny nodded gratefully. Only months later would he reflect that the punishment seemed harsh, that his share of the equity was probably worth more than one hundred and fifty-four thousand rand.

"One more thing," said Harry. "We will keep this between us. Nobody need know what you have done. Not even your children. We will keep your reputation intact, but on one condition: You agree to go into counseling."

In all the drama there was never any explanation sought, and none offered, as to *why* Ronny had stolen from them. No one thought to ask why, after thirty years of honest service, Ronny would endeavor to carry out such a crude, ill-thought-out raid on the company's coffers, one that would inevitably be discovered by the auditors and traced back to him. "Why did you do it, Ronny?" was a question that never got asked.

Jack privately surmised that Ronny justified taking the money on the grounds that he felt entitled. He was probably bitter that he was getting a third of the profits and thought he should get at least half, Jack thought. Unfortunately, a lot of employees succumbed to that entitlement perspective. It was an old story. They perceived the bosses were making money out of the sweat of their brow, and all that they were doing was taking what was rightfully theirs. Blah—blah. It was conveniently forgotten that the bosses put up the finance and took the risk in the first place. Sometimes Jack just shook his head and reflected tautologically: "Ronny stole because he has become a thief." And somehow, when you cross a line and become a thief, you can no longer distinguish right from wrong.

For a long time Harry was too hurt to even talk about it. The furthest he got as to "why?" was a half-hearted stab at "because he was probably living beyond his means." "You know, bladdy fancy house with every modcon that opened and shut."

Harry's response was to tighten their controls and to install a "mole" in the shop, an employee at manual-worker level who would secretly keep an eye on Ronny. For years the mole had nothing to report. Ronny, it seemed, had learned his lesson. Slowly, trust was being rebuilt. But one day, five years after the big theft, the mole called. Customers had been complaining that something suspicious was happening with the TV licenses, he said. This time, the amount stolen was just one thousand five hundred rand and it appeared to involve Ronny's assistant-manager, Jamal, as well. "It had been some years since the last theft," recalled Harry. "We didn't want to fire him for one thousand five hundred rand, so we reprimanded him and Jamal and let it pass."

For the next eight years there were no major incidents from downtown. Turnover was up year on year, Ronny was enjoying healthy bonuses, and things seemed to be progressing well. But then came the sickening discovery that sixty thousand rand of stock was missing.

Harry's instinct was that "Honest Ron" was behind it, and he was finally ready to give his "cheating brother" the boot. It was enough dealing with the ram raiders and scamsters that had become an endemic feature of doing business on Jules Street, he didn't also need it from his brother. But almost immediately Jamal had confessed and, despite intense questioning, he had insisted that he had acted alone. Still, Harry's anger lingered. Even if Ronny had not been involved, he had, at the very least, been grossly negligent—and damn stupid—to allow sixty thousand rand to be stolen from under his nose.

These are the events that Harry replays in his mind as he prepares to view the video footage of the mysteriously empty cash-drop box.

CHAPTER 19

Ronny Sher Takes a Polygraph

did not take it," insists Ronny, perched on the plastic chair on the plastic runner. "I swear I did not take it."

Harry homes in on Ronny. "Tell me," he pauses to let his words sink in, "how does eleven thousand rand disappear into thin air?"

"Maybe it was Maximum Security Services. Maybe they took it."

"What's wrong with you, Ronny? Are you a kleptomaniac or something? How many chances do we have to give you?"

"Harry, I swear I did not take it. Last time I took it, I admitted it. This time, I am innocent, I swear. Maybe the bank tellers took it."

"You can go and see the bank video for yourself. Here, I'll call the bank manager. You can go right now. Would you like to go right now?"

So Ronny walks over to the bank. An hour later he's back. Jack, too, is back from his haircut, his silver-gray curls neatly cropped. Jack has been going to the same hairdresser in Birdhaven for the last thirty years, and usually his return would spark some wisecrack from

Harry, but today neither Harry nor Jack are in the mood for wise-cracks. Jack leans back, a grim look on his face. Best let Harry deal with his own brother.

"Well?" says Harry.

"That big black teller in the video who opened the cash box looked like a big crook to me," ventures Ronny. "He was wearing a hood and he was whistling away. You know, it could have been him."

An extraneous detail! Harry notes this. He has been reading and studying a sleuthing book, bought for him by Carmen, called *Truth Extraction: How to Read Between the Lies.* Now he applies one of the first principles: when the respondent starts offering superfluous information—man whistling away, man wearing a funny hat—it is an unconscious indication that they feel uncomfortable with the question and are looking to lie their way out of it. He mentally ticks off other telltale signs of deception he has noticed in Ronny—his tendency to hold unnerving and unwavering eye contact for exam-ple. The book says that people who associate shifty eyes with lying will tend to overdo the fixing of eye contact, causing them to go to extreme lengths to maintain eye contact, almost to the point of rude-ness. Likewise, Ronny's tendency to tap his fingers on the chair as if you are wasting his time is another telltale sign. According to the book, when the respondent disassociates inappropriately, when they preoccupy themselves with activities such as straightening their clothing, tapping their fingers, whistling, humming, examining fin-gernails, or staring vacantly out of the window, these are sure signals that the person is finding the confrontation stressful and is uncon-sciously seeking ways to escape. Keep calm, he tells himself, keep scrutinizing his behavior, be patient and draw as much out of him as you can.

"I don't want to hear any more of your crap!" Harry explodes. "What's someone whistling got to do with anything? A guy with a funny hat who is whistling—what the hell has that got to do with anything?"

But Ronny continues to vehemently protest his innocence.

"There is only one way to settle this," bellows Harry. "Polygraph. You will have to take a lie detector test. You, and the man from Maximum Security Services. Then we'll see who's telling the truth."

Trump Polygraph is situated in a modern glass-and-brick building on a rocky promontory overlooking the satellite city of Roodepoort, a fifty-five-minute drive west of Johannesburg. Their two chief interrogators—Kevin Cronje and Luke Erasmus—have built a reputation as perhaps the toughest and most experienced polygraph testers in the greater Witwatersrand region.

Kevin, forty-seven, stocky, with small eyes and a frighteningly direct manner, is a former constable in the South African Police. Luke, thirty-four, his younger colleague, tall and slim with straight blond hair swept neatly back, served in the Special Forces of the South African Defence Force. Kevin left the police in the eighties "because there was no money in it," he says, and flew to America to study the art of polygraph at the Backster School of Lie Detection in San Diego, one of the most renowned schools of polygraph in the world. Luke's aspiration had been to become a detective, but his father dissuaded him from joining a government institution where there was "no pay and no future." So, like Kevin, he went private and joined Trump Polygraph after also graduating from the Backster School of Lie Detection.

Polygraph is an art as well as a science, the two men like to explain. And in practicing their art each of them have their strengths and weaknesses. "Kevin is better at interrogating whites," Luke begins, "whereas I tend to get better results with black people. But that is not exclusive, hey. I can also do whites."

"Ya, we've got our different methods," adds Kevin. "You could say I am more direct."

"Kevin can be very short with black people," says Luke. "But that has nothing to do with being racist."

"Ya, on the contrary," says Kevin, "some people see me as quite liberal. I was the only English-speaking policeman at my station in Pretoria. Trust me, compared to those okes, I am, like, very liberal. Trust me, I was not liked."

"I would say that Kevin is quite liberal and I am very liberal," says Luke.

Back in the eighties the odds of finding a liberal white cop and a liberal member of the army in the same room would have been slim indeed. For decades, liberals never managed to garner more than 10 percent of the white vote. But now, in the new South Africa, the collective amnesia is such that it's hard to find anyone who admits to ever having supported the apartheid regime.

Ronny arrives at Trump Polygraph a few minutes early for his 10 A.M. interview and is ushered into a waiting room. Two other women sit, arms folded defensively, looking straight ahead. Nobody talks. Nobody makes eye contact.

Presently, Luke Erasmus appears at the door, clipboard in hand.

"Ronny Sher?" he announces. Luke notices that Ronny is about two heads shorter than he is. "Follow me, Mr. Sher," he says, almost cheerily.

He leads Ronny down a corridor to the interrogation room and steps aside to let Ronny enter.

"Look here, I'm a busy man, how long is this going to take?" Ronny is immediately on the offensive, wanting to let this blond, bespectacled interrogator with Aryan features know that he is dealing with someone important . . . not your regular lowly employee. "I'm a manager. I've got a shop to run. I don't even know why I'm here."

Luke sizes up Ronny. Small-man syndrome, he thinks. He's seen it before. Small man with his forceful little way trying to act outraged. I don't care if you're big, small, smelly, or fat, he says to himself. Plenty of time to find out whether you are guilty. Luke knows that four out of five people who walk through his door fail the polygraph. They all protest their innocence, but, by the time he is finished with them, 80 percent have changed their plea.

"Please sit down, Mr. Sher," he says politely. He motions to a chair and lights up a Craven A cigarette. Then, smoke curling from his nostrils, he begins to tap purposefully on the keyboard of his laptop. "Polygraph test conducted for Jules Street Furnishers by Luke Erasmus on Ronny Sher," he types.

Ronny takes in the room: a claustrophobic booth with bare walls, and propped in the corner, a black bag with strange objects spilling out. Unknown to Ronny, a hidden CCTV camera captures his every word and movement, transmitting it to a TV screen set up in the adjacent room. Sometimes employers like to watch their employees being interrogated, but Harry and Jack have declined the invitation, and, so, today the adjacent room is empty, though the video records the process, should they later request footage.

After a few minutes of tapping away on his laptop, Luke is ready to begin the preliminary interview. "Do you know why you are here today?" he begins, his voice dispassionate.

"Yes," replies Ronny.

Luke pauses, surrounding Ronny's answer with a layer of silence before he launches into the next question.

"Are you on any medication at the moment?" he continues.

"No."

"Your health, is it good?"

"Yes."

"For how long have you been working for Jules Street Furnishers?"

"About forty years."

Now he begins to quiz Ronny in depth about the missing money. "Did you prepare the bank deposit that went missing? Can you explain, step by step, how you prepared that deposit? How much money was in that deposit box?"

And then comes the crunch question: "Did you steal the missing eleven thousand rand?"

Luke listens intently to Ronny's terse replies and—under the heading 'preliminary interview'—types up a quarter-page summary of his answers: "The subject states that he himself dealt with the money. The subject counted all the money that was due for banking . . . Once the money had been dropped, the subject had no further contact with the money. The subject denies having stolen the missing eleven thousand rand. Subject does not know what to suspect with the missing money. No further comments were noted from this subject."

Luke removes his spectacles and rubs his eyes. He has just completed the most predictable part of the test. They all deny. Now he must conduct the polygraph.

He unzips the black bag in the corner and begins to unpack its contents, laying them on the desk in front of Ronny. There is a pneumograph to measure breathing, a galvanometer to measure changes in perspiration rates, and a blood pressure cuff to measure changes in pulse rates. Ronny wriggles uncomfortably.

Earlier Luke had explained to Harry the theory behind a polygraph. What the polygraph measures, he told him, are the unconscious changes that take place in the human body in response to certain questions. Specifically the breathing rate, perspiration rate, pulse rate, and blood pressure. The word *polygraph* simply means "many writings," because it collates the results of these three systems in the human body; and then it's up to the trained polygraph examiners to interpret them. The success of polygraph is based on the theory that lying triggers an emotional and physical reaction that the individual cannot control. Although we might easily lie to others, we cannot lie to ourselves without inducing an involuntary physical response. As human beings, we were born to tell the truth. We only lie because we are fearful of the consequences of telling the truth. Will I go to jail? Will I lose my family? It's fear of the truth coming out, it's the stress of this that causes a physiological response. In the hands of skilled examiners, the polygraph is highly accurate, he assures him. Research indicates that accuracy is close to 100 percent. Only if the subject believes their lies will they go undetected.

"Sit nice and still and just answer my questions, yes or no," Luke instructs Ronny, attaching the abdominal pneumograph sensor to

Ronny's stomach. Now he straps the thoracic sensor to his chest, the blood pressure cuff to his arm, and pumps it up.

"Listen to my questions, answer yes or no, and when the test is finished I will immediately release the pressure off your arm."

Ronny nods. Luke unscrews a tube of Electro-gel, imported from the United States. "Open the palm of your hand, just sit nice and still and answer the questions, yes or no." He attaches the diode sensors of the galvanometer to the fingertips of Ronny's right hand. He speaks calmly but forcefully, and keeps on repeating the essential instructions. "Feet in front of you, look straight in front of you, listen to my questions, answer yes or no."

Finally Ronny is all strapped up and Luke is ready to begin. He tells Ronny each of the questions he will ask, articulating each question in turn. "There will be no surprise questions, no trick questions," he says. "Do you understand?"

"Yes," says Ronny.

"Were you born in South Africa?"

"Yes," says Ronny.

There is a long silent pause. Luke looks at the screen and says nothing. Ronny sits straight-backed and, breathing audibly, waits for the next question.

"Do you believe I will only ask you the questions I have told you about?"

"Yes."

Once again, in line with standard polygraph procedure, Luke leaves a twenty-one-second gap between the answer and the next question. The physiological response needs time to take effect on the scrolling graph, and to settle back before the next question. These neutral control questions are important because they give the examiner a baseline reading against which responses to the provocative questions—called red-zone questions—will be measured.

"Between the ages of fifteen and twenty, do you remember stealing something valuable from someone who trusted you?"

"No."

"Other than the missing eleven thousand rand, have you ever at any time in the past stolen money from Jules Street Furnishers?"

"No."

"Have you ever at any time in the past stolen goods from Jules Street Furnishers?"

"No."

"Did you take the missing eleven thousand rand from Jules Street Furnishers?"

"No."

Luke releases the blood pressure cuff around Ronny's arm and exits the room. A few minutes later he returns, and pumps up the blood pressure cuff. "I will ask you the same questions but in a different order," he says.

Once again, Ronny denies everything. Luke disconnects the equipment and sends Ronny on his way without a word. The brief from Jules Street Furnishers was simply to conduct a test and report the result. Luke types up his conclusion. "It is the opinion of the examiner that the subject did not answer all the questions truthfully. It is recommended that the subject be brought back for a full exit interview." He faxes it over to Harry Sher who calls to ask what the hell it means.

"He failed the test," Luke tells Harry. "But we would have to conduct further tests to know whether he is lying about the eleven thousand rand, or whether he is lying about other monies he might have stolen."

"What do you mean *other monies?*" says Harry.

"It's normal procedure to ask if they have stolen from their employer in the past. The conscience likes to unburden itself. You might be after one thing and discover another."

"And what did he reply in answer to that question about *other monies?*" says Harry.

"He said he was innocent, but his chart went crazy."

Harry is quiet a moment. "We didn't want to tell you because we didn't want to prejudice the result, but over the years Ronny has been caught with his hands in the till a number of times."

"You should have told me," says Luke. "Send him back. This time we'll get a confession."

Exactly one week later, Ronny Sher walks back into the reception of Trump Polygraph. Harry had broken the news—in trademark blunt style—that he had flunked the test, and that he had to return for a retest.

Once again Luke is standing, clipboard in hand, calling for "Ronny Sher." This time, notes Luke wryly, the forceful, pushy, small-man syndrome is not in evidence. Last time it was Ronny's conversation. This time it will be his conversation. However long it takes.

"You failed your test," Luke begins, once they are seated in the same claustrophobic room. "It is my job to find out why you failed. Now we can sit here all day. Up to you." Luke's tone is acerbic. The low-voltage, probing interviewer of the previous week has been transformed into a vicious electric drill, ready to tear holes in his subject.

"Why do you think you failed, Mr. Sher?"

"I don't know," says Ronny.

"No, no, no, let's not beat around the bush. You've taken the test, you've shown a reaction. Let me show you your chart, Mr. Sher. Look here, Mr. Sher. This question about whether you have ever taken money from Jules Street Furnishers. Why did your heart start racing? And why, when I asked you about the missing eleven thousand rand, did you stop breathing for five seconds? Is that normal? Tell me, is that normal?"

"No."

"Right! Talk to me!"

It is not long before Ronny starts to unburden himself. First, he confesses to "lending" six hundred rand. "I had intentions of paying the money back," he insists.

"Have you paid that money back yet?" asks Luke.

"No."

Next, Ronny tells Luke that he and his assistant manager, Jamal, sold batteries and pocketed the returns. Third, he admits that, once again in cohoots with Jamal, they pocketed the proceeds of TV licenses. He can't remember what the amounts were, but they couldn't have added up to much. "Petty cash," he says.

"Stealing is stealing," replies Luke. "It doesn't matter whether you steal ten rand or ten thousand rand. Now, Mr. Sher, is there anything else you would like to tell me?"

"No."

"Do you understand, Mr. Sher, that we were born to tell the truth? Do you understand that the human mind likes to confess, and that unless you clear all outside issues, you will never pass the test about the eleven thousand rand we are trying to clear up today?"

"Yes."

"Are you sure there is nothing else?"

"Yes."

"We shall see," says Luke.

Luke begins tapping on his laptop, a plume of smoke from his cigarette rising in a single spiraling column. "Preliminary interview: Subject confessed to certain issues regarding the theft of money from Jules Street Furnishers . . ." Luke lists the items confessed to. This will not be all, he thinks. Once the perimeter wall starts to crumble, it is a matter of time before the entire edifice collapses.

Now, once again, he unpacks his bag and hooks Ronny up. Once again, he tells Ronny the questions he will be asking and instructs him to simply answer yes or no. Once again he tests him, walks out, and returns to retest.

"I am afraid, Mr. Sher, that you have still not passed your test. Do you know why?"

"There was one thing I forgot to mention."

"Go on."

"Me and Jamal used to do repairs of radios. Off the books."

"How much did that involve?"

"I can't remember."

"Are you sure?"

"Yes."

"Is that all, Mr. Sher?"

Another test. Ronny loosens his tie. He starts to sweat.

"Other than what you have told me, did you steal the missing eleven thousand rand from Jules Street Furnishers?"

"No."

"Other than what you have told me, regarding the missing eleven thousand rand from Jules Street Furnishers, did you take the money?"

"No."

"Again, Mr. Sher, I have to tell you that you failed the test."

For three hours Luke interrogates Ronny, but no further confessions are forthcoming. Eventually Luke sends him packing and types up his carefully worded conclusion. "It is the opinion of the examiner that the subject did not answer all of the questions truthfully," he writes. "It is further the opinion that the subject is withholding information regarding the missing eleven thousand rand. The subject did confess to certain irregularities regarding money at Jules Street Furnishers. This did, however, not change the result of the test once the subject was retested."

Luke faxes the report over to Jules Street Furnishers, where Harry paces impatiently.

"What the hell does this mean in plain English?" Harry shouts down the phone to Luke. "The test shows he is guilty. But we cannot say exactly what he is guilty of."

"Look Luke, you have grilled him twice. You are experienced at detecting who is telling the truth and who is lying through their teeth. That is what we pay you for, right? So tell me, what is your gut conclusion? Innocent or guilty?"

"In my opinion," says Luke, speaking slowly but deliberately, "the guy is *vuil*. Definitely dirty."

CHAPTER 20

The Man at Maximum Security Services

Before Harry can do what he is itching to do, there is one piece of the jigsaw to be completed. Blame the bookkeeper in him, blame the anal company secretary who likes to dot every *i* and cross every *t*, but Harry needs confirmation from Maximum Security Services that *their* man has passed his polygraph before he can, with clear conscience, give his brother the bullet for failing his.

He calls up Maximum and asks to speak to Shane Skinner, the security officer of their Johannesburg branch. He is put on hold.

While Harry waits, he strokes his yellow tie. Today Harry is dressed in red leather shoes, orange socks, tan trousers, and an orange shirt. He's got more colors on him than the South African flag, but true to form, his socks match his shirt.

Jack is also at his desk this fine morning and on the phone to Suzette, who is laughing, telling him, "Mr. Rubin, you can't believe who's just hobbled in. *Yusses*, man, I wondered what happened to those okes. I wondered why they hadn't been returning my calls.

Veli's got his leg in plaster of paris, Obi's all strapped up, says he's got a few broken ribs. They look like a couple of extras from *ER*."

Obi and Veli, Suzette proceeds to inform Jack, were in a car accident. Apparently, Obi's bakkie had broken down and had to be towed to the garage. The mechanic told Obi that he would have to have the engine overhauled. Financially, it was a big blow to Obi—eight thousand rand—but he had no choice, since the bakkie was his income-generator, and so he dug into savings, borrowed from friends, and told the mechanic to go ahead. In the meantime, Obi and Veli used township taxis to get around, but one of these taxis took a corner a little sharply, clipped the curb, and rolled down an embankment. "One oke was killed in the *prang* [crash]," recounts Suzette. "Veli broke his leg and Obi cracked his ribs. Like, bladdy painful, man. Veli says they can start doing repos again next week."

"Good," says Jack.

Today is Thursday, Jack's golf day, and he is dressed top to toe in casual greens: light green shirt, dark green trousers, dark green socks. He leaves for the course (which at this time of year is exceedingly green, too) at 11:30 A.M. sharp to meet up with his midweek golf school. Jack has been swinging irons since the sixties. He loves the game and calls golf his therapy. He once got down to a seven handicap, which, he says, is like not bad for a twice-a-weeker. But recently, for about a year, Jack has been going through a bad patch, and his handicap has been pushed out to a thirteen, which is, like, not that good.

In the early days of Jules Street Furnishers Harry used to play, too, and for thirteen years he would partner Jack every Sunday morning at Huddle Park Golf Club, a municipal public course in the northern suburbs of Johannesburg. The two men offer conflicting accounts of just why it was that one day Harry decided he would never set foot on a golf course again.

"Golf," says Harry, "is the one game that puts you in total euphoria when you are playing well, but when you play badly, it's 'fuck it' all the way. With me, there were more fuck it days than euphoric days. I can remember enjoying about seven rounds of golf in thirteen years. The rest of the time it was purgatory. So I started to think: Do I need this in my life? Who needs this in their life? The day I gave up was one of the happiest days of my life."

Jack harbors suspicions that Sher quit because he was not as good as he was. "Sher likes to be top dog. When he's top dog, he's happy, otherwise he's grim." Also, the way Jack sees it, Sher's problem was that he took the game too seriously. "Most of the time, he walked round with a little black cloud over his head. You have to ease up, relax. Guys who are too intense never do well."

When the conversation turns to golf, Harry likes to get his jabs in first, and to this end he tells the story of how, one year, he and Jack got to the final of their golf club's Doubles Knockout Competition.

"I was a twenty-two handicap, Rubin was an eighteen," he begins. "We were playing these guys who were, like, hotshot single-figure golfers who didn't believe for one minute that we could beat them." At this point in recounting the story Harry gives a derisive sneer. "After seventeen holes we were one up. All we had to do was halve the eighteenth and we would have had a decisive mental advantage going into the final afternoon round. That was when Rubin collapsed."

"What do you mean I collapsed?" Jack counters indignantly. "I made a mistake, I didn't collapse."

"Like a pack of cards, Rubin!"

At this point in the story Jack will always try and put the matter straight. "What happened was this. I had a putt for a four to win the hole, to put us two up for the eighteen holes. Sher had putted out for a five, or so I thought, which would have been enough to tie the hole. But I'd miscounted one of Sher's shanks into the rough. In fact, he'd scored a six, so I needed to at least get down in two if I was to halve the hole. Anyway, I putted for the win and just as the ball looked like it was going to run straight into the cup, it died at the last moment and missed on the left-hand side. I just had a tap in, but mistakenly thinking that Sher had already halved the hole, I picked up my ball and started walking to the next tee. The other guys ruled we'd lost the hole."

"You could have just putted the *chazzisher* ball. You could have asked me what I scored? Why did you have to pick up the ball?"

"It was a mistake."

"No B.M.T. [big match temperament], Rubin. No B.M.T."

"Those guys if they were mensches, should have let me replace the ball and have my putt, but no, they applied the letter of the law. It put us all square for the first eighteen, and afterwards we were so devastated we couldn't recover."

"Ya, instead of wearing the winner's smile, we were wearing the runners-up's grimace. That's what I mean about golf. Most of the time it's purgatory!"

Harry is still hanging on, impatiently listening to elevator music and waiting to speak to Shane Skinner. "What's with these okes? We pay them ten grand a month and nobody's in."

———

The branch of Maximum Security Services where Shane Skinner works is situated on a side road in a gritty industrial area called Crown Mines, to the west of the southern edge of the city center. To get there from Jules Street Furnishers you have to travel the entire length of Jules Street heading west, take Main Street through the city center, and then pick up the traffic-clogged Main Reef Road on the other side. There you hold your breath against the belching lorries and articulated trucks inching forward bumper-to-bumper, until, after two miles, at the Nappy Warehouse billboard, you turn off and head toward the abandoned Crown Mines row houses, with their red tin roofs sparkling in the highveld sun. Presently you arrive at the fortified premises of Maximum Security Services, where the outer perimeter fence is electrified and supplemented by rolls of barbed wire and a uniformed security guard emerges from a hut to ask your business.

Inside the compound, the on-site security is state-of-the-art. To enter the low-rise office block, you pass through two steel-plated bulletproof doors, each door controlled by magnetic locks that are activated by an operator on the inside. Closed-circuit cameras record every movement.

Maximum Security Services is one of the three largest cash-in-transit firms in the country. Started more than sixty years ago by an Englishman who opened a small office in Hillbrow, the high-rise, high-density flatland of Johannesburg, it now has more than thirty branches and is listed as a public company on the Johannesburg Stock Exchange. Initially they had only one major client, OK Bazaars, a clothing and general goods department store, whose cash takings they would collect and bank on a daily basis. The company grew steadily, spreading its tentacles across Johannesburg and beyond. For decades Maximum Security Services drivers operated in a relatively crime-free environment. They drove ordinary vehicles and their operatives carried .38 specials, firearms that they rarely used. A vehicle was attacked perhaps once in five years.

Shane Skinner—five feet seven, weighing two hundred pounds, and built like a Humvee—is third in command of the main Johannesburg branch of Maximum Security Services. His office, down a narrow, dark corridor, is a small, dingy space, and it is from here that he directs operations. Shane's filing cabinet is stacked with "Monthly firearm reports," "Disciplinary Hearings Files," and customer files. The file of Jules Street Furnishers is buried under dozens of others with issues pending.

Between the assorted paperwork, a couple of live, full-metal-jacket bullets, .38 specials, are scattered around his desktop. Shane, twenty-seven, a self-confessed danger junkie, likes to rub the cold, smooth metal of the bullets in the palms of his hands as he talks, tossing them intermittently from one hand to the other like a juggler. "If you don't find danger exciting . . . if you don't find it thrilling, then you shouldn't be in this job," he tells his operatives. He has the scars to back up his words.

When Shane joined Maximum Security Services at the age of nineteen, elections for a democratic South Africa were imminent and the risk environment in which Maximum operated was shifting dramatically. Attacks on their cash-in-transit vans by armed gangs had become a regular occurrence, and at least four a month was the norm. Maximum's response was to bolster security: They installed armor-plated doors, bulletproof windows, and supplied escort vehicles for backup. But the armed gangs simply raised their game. Instead of holding up the crew and making off with the cash without harming anyone, they began to ambush the vehicle and shoot at it—as well as at the escort vehicle—until the driver capitulated. In 1994, when Shane worked as a driver, he was attacked no less than six times. "Gangs of robbers were standing along both sides of the road and firing at me," he recalls. "It was like I was running a gauntlet in some gangster movie. If not for the bulletproof plating, I would be dead."

Unlike some operatives who found the violence traumatizing, danger became an integral part of what attracted Shane to the job. "As a driver, your job is to defend your vehicle and deliver the money," he says. "It's a rush. It's a thrill. I never felt so alive as when I was on the job. Every day I would leave for work with the thought that I might not come home to my wife and *lightie* [child]. You have to be fearless. If you get scared, you *will* die."

One day Shane took a bullet to the stomach from a 9 mm pistol and spent a fortnight in intensive care. On his return to work, the company promoted him to a high-ranking desk job where he became responsible for the security of all his branch's cash-in-transit vehicles.

As violent crime spiraled through the late nineties, Maximum upgraded their security once again. To prevent ramming, they installed bulletproof armor in the noses of their vehicles, and they soldered on heavy-duty batter-proof bumpers at the rear. Each member of the crew was supplied with a bulletproof vest and a .38 special revolver with six rounds of ammunition. The driver was housed in a bulletproof cockpit that he was to occupy at all times. If the driver's door was opened, the whole vehicle was instantly immobilized. In addition, the back of the van was fitted with safes, and the cash-drop boxes were equipped with radio-operated die canisters.

The die canisters were particularly ingenious, meant to neutralize attacks on Maximum operatives in the vulnerable space between the shop and the vehicle. "If a robber holds up an operative and steals the cash-drop box," explains Shane, "the die in the drop box is activated as soon as the box goes out of the range of the radio signal from the homing device in the van, and at that point all the notes are stained in red dye. It makes what they steal completely useless.

"So, in order for the robbers to get away with it, they have to steal the cash-drop box as well as the homing device in the back of the van. In order to do that, they have to have inside knowledge about how the system works," says Shane.

The robbers responded by once again notching up the ferocity of their attacks. They immobilized the vehicles by ramming them head-on with BMWs specially fitted with bull-bars. Then they set about attacking them using AK-47s loaded with armor-piercing bullets. If that didn't work, they doused the vehicle with petrol and set it alight. That got the driver out pronto. "One month, we had fifteen armed holdups of our vehicles," says Shane.

Yet, the reason why so many attacks have continued to be successful, confides Shane, is that the brains behind some of the holdups are quite clearly high-ranking operatives within their own company. "The people who carry out the heist and who end up shot and killed are not the same people as the brains behind the operation," he says. "We know this because the way the robbers get into our vehicles and the way they make sure to deactivate the homing device. They are too clever, and that tells us they have inside information. Recently one of our operatives was caught organizing heists and was sentenced to fifteen years. For sure, he is not the only one."

The police, adds Shane derisively, are in on it, too. "Part of the problem is their pathetic salaries—about three thousand five hundred rand a month, a pittance. Even Maximum operatives earn more. We start off at four thousand three hundred rand, but with pension, overtime, and medical benefits, our package is worth six thousand rand.

"Look, if I am honest, I understand where they are coming from. You look around in the new South Africa and you see people minting it. And you think—why not me?"

Shane admits his attitude to crime is ambivalent, not least because it is "good for business." "We have to thank our lucky stars for the robberies of banks and of business, for without them I wouldn't have a job," he laughs. "If a business gets robbed of its daily takings, it's like the robber has done our marketing for us. We then arrive and offer to do their banking for them, and they are falling at our feet to sign the contract."

One of Shane's clients is Jules Street Furnishers, who have been with them for about eight years. In the past things have gone smoothly with this client, he says, but now there is an empty cash-drop box to investigate. The honesty of his operatives is being questioned. Each one of them will have had a polygraph on joining the company—part of their pre-employment screening—to ensure they have no criminal history. Now they will have to undergo another test. Shane believes his operatives are not responsible, because the bank teller had signed that on receipt the box seal was intact. Nevertheless, he has assured Mr. Sher that it is standard company policy that each operative who handled their cash-drop box on the day in question will be given a polygraph.

———

Now, as the call from Mr. Sher is put through, Shane must root around his cluttered desk to unearth the file for Jules Street Furnishers.

"Shane Skinner!" booms the familiar voice of Harry Sher down the line. "Okay Shane, now, you know what I'm going to ask you. Shane, remember the box from our branch that went missing. Now, what I need to know from you is this: Have your employees taken their polygraphs? Because, if I'm going to accuse my manager of theft, if I'm going to make such a serious accusation, I must be sure of where we stand. So you need to tell me, Shane, have your blokes passed the polygraph?"

CHAPTER 21

Fernando Wants Time Off

The decision as to how to deal with his brother weighs heavily on Harry. He veers between anger and despair. In his anger, he knows exactly what he will do: Fire Ronny for theft, cut ties, never see him again. Anger is Harry's friend because it brings him clarity. But when Harry evaluates the situation rationally, he knows that his preferred course of action may not be possible.

In the new South Africa, unlike the old, you can't just fire an employee who you believe has been stealing from you. There are formal procedures you have to follow. You have to have proof—polygraphs are not accepted as evidence in a court of law—or a signed confession.

"What can we do?" Harry asks Jack, pacing the plastic runner. "Do we take him to court like Jamal? Do I accuse my own brother of being a thief in a public court?" Jack leans back in his chair, menthol toothpick in hand, and nods gravely. "It's not pretty," he agrees.

For days Harry and Jack grapple with the dilemma of what to do about Ronny.

Downstairs, Fernando and Suzette are wrestling with their own problems. Suzette's husband, Jonny, who worked as an air-conditioning tradesman, has been out of a job for months and she is afraid that they will be unable to keep up the mortgage and that they might lose their house.

Fernando, too, has been going through a tough time. He has been carjacked twice and has endured an acrimonious split-up with his mixed-race girlfriend, Mina. "My nerves are like shot," he tells Suzette. "I think I am about to have a nervous breakdown."

While putting the finishing touches to the Jules Street Furnishers color Christmas catalogue, Fernando recounts to Suzette, and anyone who will listen, the escalating, unfolding drama of his life.

A year after his wife died, Fernando met Mina Malherbe, an attractive woman barely half his age and considerably slimmer than he was. They had first become entwined in a sweaty club at the Estoril Hotel in Joubert Street, not exactly the city's most salubrious nightspot, where they had danced under the strobe light until dawn. Fernando realized he was lonely, and that Mina could offer him companionship and sex, but he wasn't interested in pursuing anything serious. But then something happened that made him see that he needed her, and he asked her to move in.

"One day I go to pick up some money from a Portuguese customer who hasn't paid his account and who lives near me in Bez Valley," he begins. "I am walking up his garden path, it's a normal day, next thing I am full of blood and screaming. I never see his dog. It bites me all over. I need nine stitches in each leg. Mina, she look after me. She bathe my wounds. She make me ham and cheese sandwiches for my lunch. And a bit of fruit. She very good sandwich maker. So I let her stay."

Fernando's grown-up sons never accepted Mina, who had two grown-up daughters of her own. They cited the age gap—"she could be your daughter, Dad"—and the fact that Mina swore like a trooper. "Every second word a 'fuck,' dad." But the fact that she was mixed-race and they were white might have had more to do with it.

As long as Fernando was having fun with Mina, he was content to defy his sons. "There aren't many ladies around when you get to my age," he told them. "Leave your old man in peace." But after five years together, Fernando and Mina's relationship started to sour. Fernando would tell her, "Please, Mina. Go. Leave my house."

"No ways," she would reply, "I have nowhere to go. You need me. No ways."

Fernando kept insisting, "When I come home, I want to see you gone."

But day after day when Fernando returned from work she was still there. "When I saw that she was not gone, I get so upset that I can't even talk to her," he recalls. "But she would call me for supper, and after I ate I like her again. So I let her stay. But next morning, I ask her to leave again."

As Fernando tells it, two developments hardened his resolve. "One day Mina make me sandwiches for lunch and afterwards my stomach is in such pain like you can't believe. I begin to suspect that she maybe put something in the food. That she trying to poison me. Of course, I can't be sure, it sound crazy, but I see that Mina has become hard towards me and that I can't trust her food. I also learn that same week that she steal and crook from me. I used to give permission to buy from Edgars [a clothing department store] on my account, but then I decide to close the account because she spending too much on the Edgars credit card. A few months later I get a phone call from the manager at Edgars. "Mr. Perreira," he says, "your account is four thousand seven hundred and seventy three rand in arrears."

"What!" I say. "I closed my account months ago."

"No, your wife came to reopen your account. She brought a letter from you."

"That was the last straw. I went home and told Mina nicely, 'You fucking bitch, you a crook, you forge my signature, now take your things and fuck off from my house or I going to report you.'

"'No, I never did that,' she tells me.

"So I shoved the documents from Edgars in her face. 'What's this?'

"She broke down. 'Sorry, sorry, I going to pay you back.'

"'I don't want you pay me back. I just want you out my life.'"

The way Fernando tells it, a terrible scene ensued. He threw Mina out, physically threw her onto the street. Then he called in a locksmith to change the locks. Mina came back the following weekend at 5 A.M. when Fernando was sleeping, and when she discovered her keys no longer worked she climbed over the tin roof of the garage and tried to get in through the back door. When she discovered that was locked, too, she started shoulder-charging the flimsy door. By now, Fernando was wide awake and scared. "I thought maybe she try kill me. She screaming and swearing like a madwoman."

Fernando telephoned his sons, who roared over in their four-by-fours. Outside a crowd of concerned neighbors was beginning to gather. Meantime, Mina had knocked the door down and entered the house. She wanted her things—her clothes, her furniture, her guitar. Fernando started chucking her clothes onto the verandah. His sons could see the situation was spiraling out of control, that some-one might get dangerously hurt. They offered to load up Mina's fur-niture and take it over to her daughter's place. An hour later a merciful silence had returned to the street as Mina and her clothes and a few pathetic items of furniture turned the corner and drove out of Fernando's life.

"I walked through my house and I was pleased to see the back of her," recalls Fernando. "But then I open my guitar case—because I play classic guitar, and that precious guitar was a gift from my wife when I turn fifty and is cost twenty thousand rand—and my guitar is gone! That bladdy bitch has tricked me. She has taken my guitar, and she has left me her old guitar that has no strings."

Fernando desperately tried to get his guitar back, appealing to Mina's daughters, but to no avail. "In revenge, I report her to police for forged Edgars letter," he says. "The police open fraud case against her. Now it between Edgars and her. But it's bye-bye my guitar."

Fernando hoped that life would settle back to normal, but since Mina left he has had nothing but drama.

First he was carjacked as he opened his garage. One moment he was going about his daily business, the next there was a gun in his ribs and he was being pistol-whipped and kicked. Then they sped off with his car. Gone. Just like his guitar. Maybe it had something to do with Mina, he thought. Maybe she got her friends to rough me up. He was getting paranoid.

Harry could see Fernando was terribly shaken up, so he sug-gested trauma counseling. "Well, I don't think so, but I see how I feel," Fernando said, his hands trembling as he lit up his eighth ciga-rette in quick succession.

With the insurance money Fernando bought another car—a secondhand Honda—but it wasn't long before the carjackers struck again. In Fernando's mind, this second carjacking was also, in a convoluted way, linked to Mina's absence. He was hijacked while collecting his dinner from a Portuguese woman who ran a private dinner-take-out business from her home, and he was only there, he realized, because, since Mina left, he had nobody to cook for him. The Portuguese woman was conveniently located in St. Frusquin Street—just two streets up from Jules Street Furnishers—and she made a living cooking Portuguese dinners for private clients. For five hundred rand a month, Fernando got twenty dinners—soup followed by a main course of meat or fish—which worked out at the bargain price of just twenty five rand per meal.

"You can't even cook for yourself at that rate," says Fernando. "You see Jags and Mercs parked outside, young couples who work and have no time to prepare meals coming to pick up, because her food is Portuguese-style and it is delicious."

A fortnight ago, as usual, Fernando went to collect his dinner. He came out, put his steaming food in the trunk, when suddenly there were guns at his head, hands in his pocket, keys filched, wallet lifted, cell phone taken, car gone. But this time Fernando had installed Netstar, a vehicle-tracking device, and a quick phone call alerted the tracking company, which two hours later found his Honda abandoned in a fast food car-park. Fernando got his car back, but when he opened the trunk, his dinner had been eaten.

"That's what the hijackers do," Fernando told Harry and Jack. "They steal your bladdy car, park it somewhere and then watch from a safe distance to see if the police come. If nobody tracks the car after a few hours, they get in and drive off."

Once again Fernando is badly shaken up. He is not sleeping at night, he tells Harry, he is scared to get into his car, to get out of his car, he imagines violent hijackers lurking behind every bush. Harry again suggests that he go for trauma counseling, but Fernando dismisses it. "Well, I feel all right," he says, lighting up another cigarette. "You know, it's not so bad, I got my car back. It's my second time—I'm getting used to being hijacked."

Instead of counseling, Fernando requests a few days off to settle his nerves. Harry and Jack are not impressed. "Look Fernando, we gave you a few days off the last time. We can't give you time off every time you get hijacked. We've got a business to run."

It is hard for Fernando to press his case, for in the midst of his strife Jules Street Furnishers suffer another devastating ram-raid, their second in twelve months.

This time, the ram raiders arrive in eight vehicles. The driver of the lead vehicle connects four heavy steel chains between the security gate and the bull-bar rear bumpers of the lead vehicle and accelerates away from the shop. The pop rivets on the security gate buckle like plywood and the gate is ripped off its hinges. Then they turn round and accelerate towards the shop, using their frontal bull bars as ramming devices to smash through the toughened glass and the slamlock gates. The shop alarm pierces the night. They know they have roughly five minutes to load up before the security company arrives.

Again, it happens in the darkest hours just before 3 A.M., again they steal approximately forty thousand rand's worth of goods, and again Jules Street Furnishers is woefully underinsured. But this time it is Harry who is raised from his sleep by the conveniently-arriving-just-too-late security company.

A few hours later, at 7:30 A.M., Harry calls Jack, who is about to leave for a vacation in the Drakensberg mountains, a four-hour drive down the highway.

"Rubin," he says, "you can't believe what's happened!"

Rubin's heart drops. "Ya?" he says.

"The ram raiders again . . . everything cleared out—every hi-fi, video, TV, they took everything. The place is trashed. It's unbelievable."

"Shit," says Jack, gritting his teeth. "Can you handle it, Sher?"

"Sure," says Harry. "Enjoy your holiday."

CHAPTER 22

The Broader Picture

When, Harry and Jack often wonder, is the government going to get serious and do something to reduce the level of crime? For nearly ten years the post-apartheid crime wave has gathered pace, and although this has always been a violent society, no one, including Harry and Jack, expected crime to soar in the way that it has. Now, with no sign of it abating, they want their democratically elected government to vigorously tackle what they perceive—along with AIDS—to be their country's most urgent problem.

The daily newspapers and weekly financial news magazines that Harry and Jack read are full of comment. They warn that crime deters tourists and international investors whose dollars are critical if the economy is to grow at the rate required to create sufficient jobs to reduce poverty. Also, as Harry sees reported on the evening SABC television news, crime is the main impetus for the country's enervating brain drain. A quarter of doctors who graduated in South Africa between 1990 and 1997 have left, according to the S.A. Medical

Association, and their primary reason for doing so is neither better opportunities abroad nor disillusion with a black government, but fears for the personal safety of their families. Reducing crime, these commentators keep repeating, is critical to the country's ability to grow itself out of poverty and build a broader economic base.

As he drives between their branches, Jack listens to talk radio, where callers discuss the psychological effects. Crime has done more to spoil the "feel good" factor that followed the 1994 elections, the callers say, than any other single issue. On the weekend Jack reads a prominent article in the *Sunday Times* by a psychiatrist who sees people in his practice who are suffering, he says, from "pretraumatic stress syndrome," a sense of acute, debilitating anxiety that something *might* happen to them. The psychiatrist says everyone knows someone who has been randomly held up, and they rationally assume it is only a matter of time before it is their turn. The article is penned by Dr. Ike Ntskikelelo Nzo, son of the late Alfred Nzo, the famous former ANC secretary general. Ike expresses strong sentiments on the rise in crime, which the newspaper trails in bold type. Jack reads:

> Criminals are going to cost this country much more than apartheid did. . . . One thing that today's violent criminals have in common with the old apartheid is that they both assaulted a human being's self-esteem and self-worth. . . . The emotional and economic cost to the country that violent criminals are inflicting is going to surpass the cost of apartheid, if it has not yet done so. . . . The time has come for us to stop offering social and political excuses for the violent criminal acts where the sole motive is monetary gain for the perpetrator who knowingly disregarded the human rights of his victim.

Like Ike Nzo, Harry and Jack believe it is time the government got off the fence. But they fear the ANC are unlikely to do so. For, if the crime wave is to be construed—as many analysts believe—to be the visible element of an unofficial, undeclared war between the haves and the have-nots, it leaves the government in a compromised position. "They were elected, were they not, to be the government of the have-nots," says Jack.

But the true picture, Harry and Jack concede, is obviously more complex than this. You don't have to be sociologist, Harry says, to see that poverty and unemployment are a critical part of the story, but not the whole story. New research, published in the *Star*—sourcing the Institute for Security Studies—offers new information on who is doing the crime and the economic state of the criminals who do it. The researchers note the extent to which crime is carried out by organized gangs for whom lack of employment is not an issue. An extraordinary 40 percent of hijackers and 33 percent of armed robbers are otherwise gainfully employed, the study notes.

What's more, as crime has become entrenched in the townships, it has become part of youth culture in a way that will be difficult to eradicate. The lack of credible deterrent is also a key factor. Tackling crime means diverting resources into the police and the criminal justice system, and away perhaps from crucial social service departments such as health, housing, and education, something the government has hitherto been reluctant to do.

The inadequacy of the criminal justice system in dealing with crime has left Harry and Jack to conclude that it is up to private citizens to be their own policemen. So it is that each time they are broken into they ratchet up their security: thicker security gates, heavier locks, tougher glass, spikier rolls of electrified barbed wire, shriller alarms, more security guards. Yet the ram raiders and the scamsters still come, finding new ways of breaking down their defences. There is a frustrating sense that whatever you do to raise the bar, it will not be enough.

In the face of this no-win situation, other men of Harry's and Jack's advanced years might be tempted to quit and shut up shop. But throwing in the towel is not an option they have actively pursued. "Of course, we could simply collect our debtors book and wind down," says Jack, "but our business is worth a lot more to us as a going concern, and besides, we provide a living to our staff and feel a responsibility towards them."

The experience of Jules Street Furnishers, Harry points out, is far from unique, and is simply a microcosm of the country as a whole. For, in the rest of Johannesburg beyond Jules Street a parallel story unfolds. In the northern suburbs, people of wealth—both the new black middle-class and the white establishment—respond to the crime wave by building higher walls topped with electrified barbed wire tendrils that spiral round their houses like a double helix. They buy vicious guard dogs trained to attack intruders, they install alarms and panic buttons and CCTV cameras, they put booms at the end of their streets, they employ quick-response security companies to prowl their neighbourhood, they install security gates and they drive cars with immobilisers. In the last decade, the amount spent on private security in South Africa has skyrocketed twelvefold to twelve billion rand, more than triple the government's entire housing budget.

And yet, still the thieves come. Their level of determination to break in always seems to exceed the level of the deterrence.

The stealing from within opens up another front. In the case of

Jules Street Furnishers, the list of fraudulent former employees is now almost long enough to inspire a sonnet. (Though not as long, Harry and Jack like to remind themselves, as the list of those who remain honest.) Here, too, their response has been to bolster their systems against fraud, painstakingly closing each loophole as it is discovered. But still the fraudsters find a way, still their level of determination exceeds the level of the deterrence.

And so it is, too, in the middle-class northern suburbs where Harry and Jack live, where housewives employ maids and gardeners, often two or three, and complain that this is missing and that is missing and that these people, who they trust in their very own homes, are stealing from them. They protest, but at the same time, they are not wholly surprised. The disparity between the haves and the have-nots is stark. The haves continue to try and keep what they have, the have-nots continue to try and take it away.

It is only when the crime turns gratuitously violent that this implicit social contract is broken. It is when someone is shot and killed in the process of a robbery or hijacking, when a precious life is lost for fifty rand or a hundred rand or an easily replaceable material item such as a car, that their vulnerability and outrage soars like the mercury on a scorching highveld summer's day. Panic, anger, helplessness, and thoughts of emigration follow hard in its wake. It is then that they demand accountability and ask with personal urgency: *Who* is committing all this terrible crime? *Why?*

Harry and Jack suspect it might be something about an entrenched way of life, about the way these people have become wired. "It's a funny thing," opines Jack, "but the guys who cheat at golf, even when they are found out, even after they're kicked out of one club, they somehow get themselves into another club where they cheat again. A cheat is a cheat. A thief is a thief. They just can't stop themselves."

Like Harry and Jack, the broader public's sense of *who* is stealing from them and *why* is vague and largely unarticulated. In Jack's mind, the ram raiders, hijackers, scamsters, robbers, and crooks—most of the people responsible for South Africa's crime, except, of course, for Ronny—live in an unnumbered shack on an unnamed dusty street in a lawless, impoverished township.

In Jack's mental map of greater Johannesburg, these townships are undifferentiated blobs that lurk on the margins. There is no detail to his picture, no names to the streets, no faces to the residents. He has little idea how the place functions. It is a critical oversight because what happens on these streets directly affects the quality of life on Jules Street and for that matter, all the other streets of Johannesburg. Like most whites, Jack has derived an uneasy sense of these hulking, smoking settlements from a distance, having seen them from the highway when he exits Johannesburg and speeds, for his vacation, towards the Drakensberg mountains.

And yet, all Harry and Jack have to do to color in the picture about this unknown street is to take a forty-minute drive to visit two of their newest employees. Although the advent of the new South Africa has meant that some blacks have moved into white areas, the townships are still as unknown to 99 percent of whites as they were in the darkest days of apartheid.

CHAPTER 23

The Street Where the Carjackers Live

Kumalo Street is the notorious main thoroughfare that runs for three kilometers the length of Thokoza township. In the early nineties this street was the front line, the scene of bloody confrontations between bitter political rivals, ANC comrades and Inkatha hostel dwellers, but today Kumalo Street is witness to a confrontation of a different sort—a battle with no specific adversary, a battle against chronic poverty. The four-lane street—two in each direction—is tarred, but the roadside verges are muddy, and so the thousands of pedestrians who use the street cling to the tarmac, constricting the flow of traffic and slowing it to a crawl. Hawkers, squatters, mangy dogs, hooded gangsters, pushers, mothers with babies, barefooted urchins crowd the road at the entrance to Thokoza, engulfing cars and then parting, only to swallow up the next one, like passing shadows in a doomsday diorama.

To the right of the street are the bleak men-only hostels, dinosaurs of the apartheid era, home to some of the poorest and most desperate men in the country. The sprawling Madala Hostel

runs for blocks—one of three Inkatha hostels—its low, hulking barracks like compound houses male migrant workers in conditions
more suited to stabling horses than people. The grounds inside the
walls are littered with the fly-infested carcasses of cows and goats
that have been killed and eaten and left to rot in the open air. Obi
and Veli bought their guns there, but even they will venture there by
daylight hours only.

Apart from the occasional general store and liquor store, there is
precious little commercial activity along the street's flanks. The real
shops with the real jobs are in the white areas, in nearby Alberton and
its industrial adjunct, Alrode, and further afield in Johannesburg.

As Obi and Veli ease their bakkie through the parting crowd,
they are warmly greeted by people they know. They offer a lift to
Patrick Malinga, a lackadaisical young man in his twenties who they
know to be a car thief. Patrick used to work as a reservist at the
Thokoza police station, but in 1997 he lost his job and so he started
hijacking cars because he was "hungry," he says, and because friends
invited him to join.

"Okay," he says, "I tell you our secret. There is a thing we call
TV time. At 6:30 P.M. we know that white people like to watch the
soap called *Isidingo*. It's very popular. They come home, park their
car—often outside the house because they are waiting for other people in the family to park first in the driveway so they can be the first
to leave in the morning. So while they are watching *Isidingo* and
their car is outside, we come and we hot-wire it, and then we deliver
it to our buyer who lives in Germiston. The other time we like to
work is between midnight and three in the morning, when the cars
are inside the driveway, and everyone is sleeping, and we must first
crowbar the gate."

"We can steal up to two cars a week. It depends, there are four of us, and we steal when we need money or when orders come in. This week I have not been stealing, because my younger brother was killed, and in my religion, when somebody close to you dies, you don't work for ten days out of respect. The ten days finish tomorrow. I have to pay for the burial and to put food in my fridge, so, this weekend I will steal."

Patrick's cell phone rings. He fumbles in his pocket and pulls out a gun, followed by his phone. "It's the Indian forward man for the white guy phoning to place an order," he explains, talking behind his hand. "Okay, no problem, I'll deliver early next week. . . . It's for a trailer," he grins. "For that I get about one thousand five hundred rand."

Patrick has lost count of how many cars he has hijacked, he says, twirling his gun around his forefinger. "People in the township know that I steal. The old people don't like it, but the youngsters respect people like me. They call us *the phanda*, [township] slang for people who know how to get ahead in life, how to operate." Patrick says the adulation he receives helps him brush aside occasional stirrings of guilt. He has grown used to the comforts afforded a car thief, and it has become what he knows.

"What started as one thing has become another. A job for my belly has become my lifestyle," he says, pointing to his expensive leather boots, pressed trousers, and button-down blue cotton shirt. "Look, I am no worse than the government. This government is corrupt. The only difference between me and them is that I steal small amounts. They're stealing, we're stealing . . . who is worse?"

Veli drops off Patrick at the liquor store and pulls up outside a house on Ndebele Street, a quiet residential road a couple of twists and turns off Kumalo Street. From the roadside, Ndebele Street looks respectable. Despite the stench of sewage running down the gutter the entire length of the street (*"Aish,* poo water! The drains must be blocked again!" exclaims Veli), the houses are set on small, ordered plots, each one with a number and a post box, and they are built of either brick or cheaper breeze-block cement. Some are neatly painted and well kept up, others are more derelict. The street has lights, the houses have electricity, and some of their postage-stamp front lawns are green and well maintained.

It is when you venture around the back of these houses that a whole underworld presents itself, revealing the hidden hierarchy of life in the township. The mudflat backyards have been turned into mini squatter camps, with interlocking warrens of corrugated-iron shacks. Each shack is rented out to tenants by the owners of the brick houses.

Veli lives with his girlfriend and their three daughters, aged fourteen, ten, and six, in one such shack. He pays the owner of the main house—who works as a taxi driver—eighty rand a month. Many of the owners of these houses, says Veli, have no jobs and get by on renting out rooms in their backyards.

Veli's shack—measuring just four meters by four meters—is a single windowless room with a leaking corrugated-iron roof. It is stiflingly hot in the summer, freezing cold in the winter, and floods when it rains. Inside, every claustrophobic inch is accounted for. There is a double bed on which Veli and his girlfriend sleep (their three children sleep on the lap of floor around it), and pushed up against the walls are the bare essentials of survival: a wooden trunk for their clothes; a cabinet for pots and pans, a fridge (empty except for three oranges and a chicken); a hot plate that doubles as a heater; a radio; and a TV.

Obi's house on nearby Mpele Street, where he lives with his mother and son, is a different proposition. The street itself is not unlike Veli's—residential, quiet, with a similar mix of houses—but Obi lives in the main brick-and-concrete house. His house, which is tiled throughout, has ornate wooden ceilings, a dining room with a dining-room table, a kitchen with a kitchen table, a living room with a sofa and a television, a bathroom with toilet, and two bedrooms—and it is clean and immaculate.

One of the striking features of Mpele Street is that—despite it being midmorning and midweek—most of the adults appear to be at home.

"About five hundred people live on my street, and of them, maybe only forty have a real job," says Obi.

"In my street," adds Veli, "maybe ten are working."

Here in Thokoza the unemployment rate is around 80 percent, say Obi and Veli. At first this shockingly high rate seems hard to square with the official national unemployment rate of 27 percent, or even the more credible unofficial rate of around 50 percent. It's only when you step back to consider that the latter rates are averages, arrived at by aggregating areas of near-zero unemployment, such as the northern suburbs of Johannesburg, with impoverished areas, like Thokoza, that you begin to appreciate how the national unemployment statistics conceal as much as they reveal.

Against this background of nearly full unemployment, a parallel morality takes root. But not all residents respond to the scarcity of jobs by turning—as Patrick the car thief has—to crime.

———

In between carrying out repossessions for Jules Street Furnishers, Obi and Veli like to hang with their old comrade friends—Petrus, Fanie, Bfana, and Siphiwe—who can be found most days drinking lager and shooting the breeze in Petrus' driveway near Mpele Street. Back in the eighties and early nineties, Petrus led an ANC cell in Thokoza, of which Obi was a member. "Petrus is a brilliant man," says Obi. "If he continued at school, he would have been a doctor or a scientist. He used to help us with our maths and physics. But he was also a coward. He didn't put himself in danger. He would send us."

On this particular morning, the gang is gathered as usual, lying back on empty beer boxes.

"More Hansa?" asks Petrus, pulling two bottles out of the fridge in his yard from where he runs his *spaze* shop.

"Ya," says Fanie. "It's on credit, I'm going to pay you next week."

"Next week never comes," Siphiwe laughs. He wears a floppy yellow hat, Air Nike sneakers with no laces and no socks, and strums an acoustic guitar.

"No, it comes," says Fanie, "it comes."

Fanie, the only one of the four with a regular wage-earning job, is a prison officer for Correctional Services. Today he's working the late shift.

"Hey, careful Fanie, you don't want to arrive drunk now," teases Petrus.

"They don't care—one drunk boy doesn't make a difference," says Fanie.

Until recently, Bfana also had a job, earning three thousand rand a month working in a fruit factory, but the work is seasonal and this is the off-season, he says. Petrus tries to squeeze a living out of selling beers and cold drinks from his backyard. When money gets tight, he takes the train to the sugarcane plantations in Natal where he buys a stash of marijuana—"ten rand an envelope"—usually paying the planters in kind by trading old shoes and clothing. Siphiwe sometimes accompanies Petrus on these trips. He plays a mean guitar, and, together with Petrus, has formed a band for which he has high hopes; but as yet, no gigs.

Patrick the car thief, and others like him, have tried to recruit Petrus and Siphiwe to their criminal activities. But Petrus takes an outspoken moral stand. "I am totally against crime," he says. "I didn't fight for freedom from apartheid to become a petty thief. Anyone with half a brain can see that, in the long run, crime does not pay."

"You trade in illegal drugs," Veli challenges him, defending the car thief.

"Aah, but marijuana is not a crime," Petrus insists, grinning broadly. "It's a herb. Selling marijuana is no different to selling beer."

"I draw the line at violent crime," adds Siphiwe. "We've had enough violence here to last a lifetime. But we are also human beings. We must find a way to live."

As Fanie cracks open another beer and Siphiwe strums his guitar, the men reminisce about the days when Petrus was their ANC commando leader and they were the Comrades Self-defense Unit, armed with AK-47s, fighting Inkatha on Kumalo Street. "And not just Inkatha," Bfana corrects them. "The apartheid government, the army and the police, who were getting Inkatha to do their dirty work."

"Clint Eastwood was my best soldier," Petrus says, pointing his beer bottle at Obi. "You and Siphiwe, my sharpest shooters."

"Clint Eastwood always got his man," mocks Veli, flashing a grin. They crack up laughing at the memory of "Clint Eastwood"— Obi's former nickname.

The talk shifts to their absent comrades who died in the shoot-outs. "We are supposed to be fifteen here today, not six," reflects Petrus. "My *spaze* shop would be sold out!"

"While we blacks were fighting each other and killing each other the white people were getting richer," says Siphiwe.

"Ya, we gained nothing from killing each other," nods Petrus.

"That's not true," says Bfana. Things have improved in the new South Africa."

"Ya, it's true, things have improved," Petrus nods.

"There used to be just shacks here. Now many people are getting real houses," continues Siphiwe. "We can even go to the same schools as whites. Mandela made many changes. Good changes. Now we have Mbeki. I like him, but I don't believe in him like I believed in Mandela. The problem is—no jobs."

"It's because all the big companies are still owned by the whites," says Petrus. "Most of the whites do not favor real democracy. They are pretending. They will share power, but not money. I feel angry at white people. But also, I don't want to end up like in Rwanda [the ravaged country in Central Africa where rival ethnic groups, Hutus and Tutsis, infamously massacred each other]. Our children would suffer even more. So I don't act on my anger."

"I am still waiting for my black empowerment," Bfana laughs ruefully.

Petrus shrugs. "Black empowerment is just a myth for most of us, a Romeo and Juliet story you read about in newspapers. Many of our comrades have turned to crime. A family of six, no one working, what can you do?"

"Ya, it's not easy," says Siphiwe. "I'm twenty-two. If I want a job in the new South Africa I must have qualifications."

"We thought this government would give us employment, or even training," says Obi.

"Ya, even training," echoes Siphiwe, "so we could get qualifications."

"But we got nothing." Petrus's tone hardens. "It's like we fought for freedom, and then we were dumped."

"The [ANC] politicians bought their Mercedes Benz and they forgot about us," says Siphiwe.

"Ya, but you can't only blame the politicians," says Petrus. "The white people dominated for a long time. We have to be patient. It will take time, maybe thirty years."

"No!" retorts Siphiwe angrily. "Five years. I'm giving them five years. In the meantime, it's every man for himself."

"They forgot about us," Bfana adds quietly.

"Ya." Petrus nods, resigned. "It seems like the government has forgotten about us."

Fanie says his good-byes and leaves, weaving his way, a little unsteady on his feet, to hail a township taxi to his job at the prison. Veli disappears to the end of the driveway, unzips his fly, and relieves himself on the road. Siphiwe resumes strumming on his guitar, humming a gently melody, deep in thought. Suddenly he stops, a moment of clarity creasing his brow. "The whites," he says, "they complain that people are stealing from them. But we had our lives stolen from us. We had our futures stolen from us. Apartheid was a crime for which no one has paid the price."

A contemplative silence settles over the driveway. A gust of wind whips in from the north blowing sand in their eyes and causing them to protectively cradle their beers. "The question is," Petrus says after a while. "What is crime? If you steal something from someone who has stolen from you, is that crime? Or is that justice?"

CHAPTER 24

Time Up

There is only so long you can dance on the lip of a volcano. After weeks of vacillating, Harry decides to take his chances with the labor laws. He wants to fire Ronny and lay a charge of theft. "Let *him* take *us* to court if he doesn't like it," he tells Jack.

But Jack has an alternative proposal. One of Jack's sons-in-law has suggested that Harry and Jack might find it helpful to seek the counsel of his rabbi, a man steeped, he says, in the moral way to resolve disputes and dilemmas.

Jack, who is culturally observant, though not religious, has given the matter some thought. "You know, Harry, it's not a bad idea," he says. "The rabbi might help us to get another handle on it. What harm can it do?"

The rabbi greets them like long-lost friends, engulfing each one in his ample embrace, and then settles back to listen intently to their story. When they are done, he asks a few pointed questions to establish the history of Ronny and the context of the events described.

He says he knows the family and mentions that Ronny's eldest son is a member of his congregation.

"In Judaism," he says, momentarily deliberating, "a brother who steals from a brother commits one of the worst crimes. The fact that he has done it before, that you caught him and then gave him another chance. . . ." He shakes his head. "He has abused your trust. You want to be a mensch, but it is clear you can no longer work with your brother."

Harry nods.

"On the other hand," continues the rabbi, "you can't send your brother to jail. You will be creating a scandal in the community and a public humiliation. It's not good on him and it's not good on you."

Harry and Jack murmur their agreement.

"So . . . what I suggest you do," continues the rabbi, "is that you ask him to resign. Give him financially what he is entitled to, no more, no less. And let him go."

As soon as they get back to Jules Street Furnishers Jack calls Ronny and asks him to come to the shop. Two hours later Ronny and his eldest son, Theo, a business school graduate in his thirties, troop up the stairs and rattle the slamlock security gate.

Two plastic chairs are waiting. Harry is impassive. He tells Ronny and Theo about their conversation with the rabbi—and that they have decided to follow his advice. "This is what we are going to do," Harry says calmly. Then he proceeds to lay out their terms.

Ronny listens but says nothing. His face is expressionless. He does not fidget. He makes no eye contact.

"Well," begins Theo, when Harry has finished. "My father says he did not take the missing eleven thousand rand. You want him to go, okay, but what is my father going to get out of this?"

"Your father get out of what?" says Harry, his voice rising. "He'll get what he's entitled to. That's all he's going to get."

"I mean, what sort of payoff are you offering," says Theo, confidently holding Harry's glare. "What about his pension? If you kept him on the payroll another ten months, he would be entitled to his pension. Either you give him his pension, or you keep him on the payroll another ten months."

"Keep him on the payroll! Maybe, Theo . . . maybe you didn't hear me right. What he's entitled to is his provident fund, that's it, which if I'm not mistaken comes to one hundred and fifty thousand rand. Even that—I'll have you know—we contributed half. He's lucky we're offering him that!"

"Is that all? Is that all you are offering?"

"Theo," says Harry, his voice going deathly quiet, "let me ask you something: Who has been doing the stealing around here? Me? Or him?"

" 'Him' is your brother."

"No, Theo. You got it wrong. Biologically he might be my brother . . ." Harry pauses, ramming his words home, addressing Theo, but speaking to Ronny. "What he's done is not what a brother does to a brother. And Theo, you go ask the rabbi: If a brother steals from a brother, how is it regarded? He will give you the answer. A brother who steals from a brother commits one of the worst crimes. And that is my answer. I am so *furious*. I cannot look at him. When this is over, I never want to see him again. Never want to talk to him again. A brother does not steal from a brother."

Ronny is still looking down. Not a single word has issued from his lips. "We will go away and think about it," says Theo.

"You go and you think," says Harry, stubbing his forefinger in

Theo's direction. "But if we don't hear from you by tonight, we'll see you at the arbitrator's hearing tomorrow. I took the liberty of arranging the hearing just in case. It's set for 10 A.M. Because, as you know, Theo," Harry is snorting like a bull now, "under labor law, your father is entitled to a hearing before we fire him. And after that we'll go to the police and have him arrested. So you phone, or we'll see him at the hearing. And if he doesn't attend, it will be worse for him."

Ronny and Theo hurry down the stairs and out onto Jules Street.

Some thirty minutes later Jack receives a call from Theo. "My father accepts the offer," he says tersely.

"I want a signed letter of resignation before 9 P.M. tonight," replies Jack. "A signed letter delivered in person, or we'll see you at the hearing."

Harry turns to Jack. "The bastard. Just shows how guilty he is. If he was innocent he would have taken his chances at the hearing. If he was innocent, why did he fold so quick?"

CHAPTER 25

Poetic Justice

It is a few months before Harry and Jack discover that they may have fired Ronny for the wrong thing.

It dawns on them gradually, and even then only as a side issue, as a new drama unfolds: A second cash-drop box—this one involving a deposit made by Suzette for six thousand seven hundred and sixty-one rand—turns up at the bank empty.

Harry and Jack are devastated. It seems incomprehensible to them that Suzette—now their longest-serving and most trusted employee—could have taken the money.

"Ronny is one thing," Harry says. "But Suzette! No way!"

"We have never had a problem with her—ever," agrees Jack. "I'll put my head on a block."

But theft is theft, and it has to be investigated. And so, once again Harry heads west down Jules Street to the bank, where he is treated to a private viewing of a soundless, green-streaked video. Despite the poor tape quality, it shows, quite incontrovertibly, a teller opening a clearly numbered cash-drop box, holding it up to the camera, and vigorously shaking it to indicate that it is empty.

Next comes the painful part. Harry has to broach the matter with Suzette, the member of staff of whom he and Jack are perhaps most fond. When Harry thinks of Suzette, the words that roll off the tongue are "hard-working," "honest," "bladdy funny," "excellent rapport with customers," "able to talk to anyone." Shit! He says to himself. This cannot be happening.

He is apologetic but to the point. "The bank manager has just called to say that a cash-drop box has turned up empty, Suzette; that six thousand seven hundred and sixty-one rand is missing."

"What?" exclaims Suzette.

"I am sorry to have to put you through this," continues Harry, "but since the deposit was signed off by you . . ." Harry clears his throat. "I don't want to ask. But you will understand, Suzette, that as part of the procedure when something like this happens, that I have to ask you: Did you take it?"

Suzette sits open-mouthed, her eyes filling with tears, still digesting the shocking new information. Before she can respond, Harry dives in again. "Look, Suzette, I just want you to know that if you did take it, I want you to know that we will work something out. But it will be better for you if you tell us now . . . if you come clean sooner, rather than later."

Suzette strenuously denies she has taken the money. She looks Harry straight in the eye and says that the money was deposited by her in the normal way and that it was there the last time she looked. She is composed now but Harry can see the hurt beginning to manifest. As a parting comment, she tells Harry that he might want to investigate a problem she has picked up recently with the cash-drop boxes. She has noticed, she says, that when the Maximum Security Services operative removes the box, he sometimes battles to get it out and has to bang it about. "The box used to slide out smoothly, but now it's as if something is getting stuck. Maybe there is some problem with the boxes that explains all this?" she says.

Once again, Harry calls up Shane Skinner at Maximum Security Services to tell him about the empty cash-drop box and to ask him to have the operative who collected the box investigated.

"Are you sure those boxes are impregnable, Shane?"

"Mr. Sher, you saw the bank video. Was the box sealed when it arrived?"

"Yes, but Suzette mentioned to me a problem with the drop box. . . ."

"Mr. Sher, I'm not saying that you shouldn't look to the future. Your cash-drop boxes are old and we have newer models now. More expensive, more reliable. Many of our clients have installed our new, improved boxes. I'm not saying the old ones give trouble. . . ."

"What sort of trouble, Shane?"

"Just that they're more bashed up, nothing more than that."

Harry presses Shane for more information about the old-model drop boxes, but he keeps his answers vague. He won't be drawn, especially when liability for a missing seven grand is at stake. After a while Harry backs off. "I'll think about your suggestion of new boxes," Harry says. "But you better arrange for your man to have a polygraph."

Meanwhile, Harry arranges for Suzette to visit Trump Polygraph. Harry explains that it is within her rights to refuse to take the test, but that if she pursues that option it won't look good. "I have nothing to hide," says Suzette. "I'll take the test."

After a brief preliminary interview, Luke Erasmus hooks her

up in his smoke-filled room and delivers his standard set of questions, his voice cold and emotionless. He hooks her up to the electrode sensors which measure her breathing, perspiration, and heartbeat.

Some ninety minutes later Luke is ready to compile his report. "Polygraph test conducted for Jules Street Furnishers on Suzette Fish by Luke Erasmus," he heads it. "Target issue: to determine if the subject stole the missing six thousand seven hundred and sixty-one rand. Subject confessed to the following in pre-interview: subject has borrowed eighty rand from the company without the knowledge or permission of management, and paid it back at a later stage. Subject denies having stolen the missing six thousand seven hundred and sixty-one rand from Jules Street Furnishers."

He heads up the next page "Results" and carefully consults the charts. He takes another drag on his cigarette and types: "The subject was tested and 'reacted' to the following question: 'Other than what you have told me about, did you steal the missing six thousand seven hundred and sixty-one rand from Jules Street Furnishers?' Subject answered 'No.'" Below that he pens his conclusion: "It is the opinion of the examiner that the subject has still not revealed all irregularities regarding money at Jules Street Furnishers."

He faxes his report through to Harry.

"All this vague bloody mumbo jumbo again," mumbles Harry, calling him up. "Luke, man, what are you trying to say?"

"The test indicates," says Luke, picking his words carefully, "that she's not telling us the whole truth."

"Shit!" says Harry loosening his tie. "Shit!" he repeats, white-faced. "Shit man, don't tell me!"

"Look," says Luke, "it might help to test her one more time. Get her to come in next Friday."

This time Harry and Jack are less inclined to accept Luke's verdict at face value.

"We have never, Rubin—not once—ever had a problem with Suzette."

"You know, Sher, this Luke chap, maybe his test is biased. Maybe there is an inbuilt presumption towards guilt. There are reasons why these things are not admissible in a court of law."

"It could be something with those drop boxes, Rubin. Suzette mentioned that sometimes they don't close properly."

"Because my gut feeling, Sher . . . I would put my head on a block that Suzette is innocent."

"Not so fast, Rubin. Don't make with the wild statements. Polygraph measures how you sweat and shake. It's deep unconscious stuff. We know that Suzette's husband is out of a job. Financially, she's under pressure. Worried she might lose her home. The human being is frail."

"Even the best of us."

"You know what it says in that book I was reading?"

"Ya?"

"That, as we know only too well, Rubin, the staff who have been with you the longest are the ones you can trust the least. They know the system."

"Well, one thing is for sure, Sher, *somebody* has taken the money. It didn't just disappear into thin air."

Shane Skinner phones Harry the next day to say that his operative has passed his polygraph. With a growing sense of foreboding,

Harry calls Suzette to say that she will have to return to Trump Polygraph for a retest. Suzette is indignant. Her husband, Jonny, angrily phones up an hour later: "What's this rubbish you are saying to Suzette?" he says. "She has told Luke Erasmus she is innocent. She has told you she is innocent. What more do you want? I am putting my foot down. She is not going for another test. Do you have any idea of the stress this is putting us under?"

"I understand," says Harry, feeling flushed. "We are not saying that she is guilty. We don't think she took the money. As you know, we have the utmost confidence in her honesty. The utmost, Jonny. But the investigation must take its course. She can choose not to go, of course. But it won't look good, Jonny. It will look like she's trying to hide something."

A pall settles over Jules Street Furnishers. Suzette feels violated. Harry and Jack feel terrible for pursuing one of their most trusted employees, yet confused as to where to turn. Seven grand is missing. Someone must have taken it. The polygraph points to Suzette. Their instincts say otherwise. The three of them can hardly look at each other.

Then, a few days later an unexpected show of honesty by a Maximum Security Services operative, Elias Tobias, illuminates everything. Elias has come to pick up the cash-drop box from the safe in the wall when he calls Cain Radebe, the security guard, positioned as usual on his tree stump, truncheon dangling, outside the shop.

"Come and see this," he says.

Cain ambles over, whereupon Elias holds up the cash-drop box. The flap is open and unfastened, not sealed as it is meant to be, allowing Elias to lift the lid and remove the money, wrapped in a bag, on the inside. He picks up the money and holds it in the palm of his hand.

Cain calls Suzette, and Elias repeats the procedure for her to see. "Jarra!" she exclaims.

"There are problems with some of these old boxes," Elias says casually. "You think they are closed, but they are not closed."

In a state of excitement, Suzette fetches Harry, who immediately phones Shane Skinner. "Shane, there is something I urgently want to show you," he says.

When Shane Skinner arrives with his two sidekicks the following morning, Harry, Jack, and Suzette are waiting. They lead him upstairs where they sit on one of the repossessed lounge suites.

"Tea, Shane?" says Harry.

"No thanks, Mr. Sher."

Harry now recounts—in blow-by-blow detail—the events of the previous day. Suzette then tells the story again. And Cain is called up to give his account as well.

Shane starts talking about the new, updated boxes. "I'm sure I mentioned them to someone at your head office," he says.

"If the old boxes are not foolproof," interrupts Jack, "why were we not told? If we had known the boxes were faulty, we would never have retained them."

"No, they are safe," Shane backpedals, "but they are the old model, and spares are hard to come by. About 10 percent of our clients are still using the old drop boxes because they are cheaper and they don't want to pay more. Maybe this open box situation that happened yesterday was a freak occurrence. Or maybe your manager didn't put the money in right."

"Why don't we go downstairs and try it again?" suggests Harry.

They gather round and watch—Harry, Jack, Shane, and his two sidekicks—as Suzette takes the cash takings, together with a signed deposit slip, drops them into a plastic bag that she seals and then places in the slot on top of the drop box. She then pushes the lever, the sealed bag falls with a *clunk* into the container inside the drop box, and she pulls back on the lever, all in one fluid motion.

Shane nods, indicating that he is satisfied with the procedure, and the six of them walk out of the shop and onto the street to the hole in the wall where the cash-drop box is accessed from the outside. Now Shane's sidekick takes his bunch of keys, selects one, bends down, inserts it, and opens the safe. He pulls out the cash-drop box.

And lo and behold, the flap is open. The lid falls back to reveal the cash lying in naked splendor for all to see—and remove if they have the inclination to do so.

"You know what this means, Shane! You know what this means about exactly who is guilty of stealing the missing six thousand seven hundred and sixty-one rand?" shouts Harry, tugging on his cuffs, the way he does when he wants to emphasize a point. "We have put our manager through the ordeal of a polygraph when this shows clearly that the boxes are defective and that your operative must have stolen the money. We will expect you to reimburse us fully for the missing six thousand seven hundred and sixty-one rand, as well as the cost of the polygraph."

"Of course, Mr. Sher," says Shane. "Of course. We will trace down which operative collected the money on that day."

"Not *collected* the money, Shane, *stole* the money. Let us be quite clear about that."

"Of course, Mr. Sher, of course."

"That was the best sight I've ever seen," Harry tells Jack later. "Man, oh man, did you see his face, Rubin? There it was, the cash, staring up at us, clear as daylight. What could Skinner say? I could have cried, man! I wanted to give Suzette a hug. I was just so happy!"

Jack grins, his ears reddening with pleasure, and leans back in his chair. "Did I not say I'd put my head on a block that Suzette is honest?"

Harry smoothes his tie. "Did I not say, Rubin, that it had something to do with those crappy drop boxes?" He walks up and down the plastic runner, pumped up, punching the air with glee. "Geez, you're tight, Rubin. Give a man his due!"

In the days that follow, a guilty—though fleeting—thought occurs to Jack: Does this mean that Ronny didn't steal the eleven thousand rand after all? Does this mean they fired Harry's brother for something he didn't do? That the cash-drop box in the downtown branch was faulty, too, and Ronny was innocent?

But Harry and Jack don't talk about it much, because, either way, their verdict is that Ronny is guilty. Whatever specific crime they did or did not fire him for, their perspective is that in the end he deserved what he got.

"Ronny innocent?" snorts Jack, whenever the subject is raised. "He may have been innocent that time. Maybe . . . we will never know. But that guy stole more from us than anyone else. He deserved to be fired."

"He just couldn't stop stealing," agrees Harry.

"Had his hand in the till whenever we turned our back. Good riddance, I say. And none too soon."

"It's what they call poetic justice," laughs Harry. "After all those years of deceit, we fire him for the one thing he *didn't* do."

Two months later, Harry is assuming his usual lunchtime posture, head bent over *The Citizen* while devouring his roast beef and gherkin sandwich when suddenly he gives a startled *harrumph!* "Rubin, have you seen this?"

"Ja?" says Jack, looking up from his wet cheese-and-tomato roll.

"Shane Skinner has been arrested!"

Harry straightens the newspaper with a loud snap and reads aloud from page six:

"Two security guards, who allegedly conspired to commit a cash-in-transit heist, were refused bail in the Johannesburg Regional Court yesterday. Shane Skinner (twenty-seven) and Mark Retief (twenty-two) were ordered to remain in custody until August 23 when they will reappear with their co-accused. They were arrested after police, acting on a tip-off, ambushed the gunmen at Devland in Johannesburg on July 31. Three of the gunmen were killed in the shoot-out. Seven others, including Mr. Skinner and Mr. Retief, were subsequently arrested, while two people are still being sought. Policeman Inspector Jacques Marais of the Serious and Violent Crimes unit testified that Mr. Skinner and Mr. Retief were involved in the planning, but were not present at the failed heist. Mr. Skinner has been suspended from Maximum Security Services and Mr. Retief has been placed 'on leave' by the Reliant Security company while in custody."

Jack gives a low whistle. "Well I never," he says coolly. "Our good friend, Mr. Skinner."

Harry finishes his sandwich, wipes his mouth on a paper napkin, closes the newspaper, folds it neatly, pushes it to the corner of his desk, and returns to the task at hand. He continues to diligently check and aggregate creditor's invoices on his Casio ticker tape adding machine. *Clack-clack-clack,* he punches in the numbers. Jack returns to desk-checking and approving the layout of their new, color Christmas catalogue, the first draft of which has been prepared by Fernando. "Christmas means Jules Street Furnishers time—See Jules Street Furnishers now for easy terms—Jules Street Furnishers, it's *your* home," says the top of the four-page catalogue in bold red-and-green type. As Jack hones the copy, he whistles a familiar tune.

When the saints, oh when the saints, oh when the saints go marching in, I want to be in that number, when the saints go marching in . . .

The sun slants in through the slit vertical blinds, making dancing geometric patterns of light and shadow on the wall. The fax machine plays its reassuring signature tune and spews out a constant stream of credit references. Phones ring.

Downstairs, Suzette and Fernando direct operations while their team of laid-back saleswomen serve customers. Jamal has been in to pay his regular monthly one thousand rand installment as directed by the court order. Obi and Veli arrive with a screech of burning rubber and with a repossessed sofa roped onto the back of their bakkie. Suzette takes one look at the state of it—covered in grime and filth—and declares: "*Jarra!* What do these people do with their sofas?"

Relations between Harry, Jack, and Suzette are reassuringly heading back to normal, though they took a knock in the immediate aftermath of the missing cash debacle. Initially, Suzette was deeply hurt that Mr. Sher and Mr. Rubin could even begin to suspect her. But she felt much better when they vigorously assured her that they had never seriously doubted her honesty, and that putting her through the polygraph was regrettable, but something they had to do, if only to clear her name. Maximum Security Services had duly refunded Jules Street Furnishers the stolen six thousand seven hundred and sixty-one rand plus the cost of the polygraphs, and Harry and Jack had given Suzette a check for one thousand rand as a gesture of apology and compensation for her ordeal.

As for Ronny, Jack had bumped into him quite by chance at a northern suburbs restaurant. But before they came face to face, or any words could be exchanged, Ronny took a quick detour around some side tables and sidled out. Ronny's wife, Louise, gave Jack the mother of all dirty looks. "It was like I was the guilty party!" Jack told Harry at work the next day. Harry snorted. "I'll never understand. If you're not happy working for someone, and you're an honest person, you go work somewhere else. You don't stay, you don't steal. . . ." Jack is of the opinion that their relationship with Ronny will never be reestablished. "Harry is so deeply hurt that his brother kept stealing from him that I don't think there is any possibility of reconciliation," he says. "There is no contact whatsoever with Ronny, and I don't think there ever will be."

There is welcome news, however, on the bad debts front. Their accountant has reported that the rigorous credit check procedures put in place after the Pie Shop scam, as well as the use of garnishee orders—whereby a court order is used to take (or garnish) monthly payments from overdue debtors directly from their salary checks—have paid dividends. Bad debts are down to a much more tolerable 12 percent of turnover, still two percentage points above what the furniture industry would regard as an acceptable level, but nevertheless an enormous improvement.

Out on Jules Street, Cain, the security guard, is positioned on the stump as usual, truncheon dangling. From here he looks out, as he does every day, over the heads of the barefoot hawkers to the sparkling, newly washed cars of Mr. Sher and Mr. Rubin. Heavy garage music—*doef, doef*—spills out from the next-door sports cafe. Smoke drifts up from the corner and carries with it the enticing smell of curried meat, as Princess Nzo and her competitor, Sipho Mfolo, prepare dishes for the lunchtime rush from the factory workers to the south of the street. African taxis hoot and stop suddenly and without warning to disgorge or pick up new customers. It is one of those clear, brilliant, sapphire-blue Johannesburg days, and Cain's view extends in a symmetrical V towards the impressive skyscrapers that delineate the Johannesburg city center skyline, nearly six kilometers away. As a security guard, Cain likes the straightness of the street. He finds it reassuring. You can see exactly what's coming at you. You can see exactly where you stand.

Inside, at precisely two minutes before 3 P.M., Beauty climbs the stairs to the floor above. She walks slowly and deliberately past the carpet samples and the banks of Edblo mattresses sealed in plastic, past the stacks of Panasonic TVs, Kenwood hi-fis, Defy washing machines, and Electrolux vacuum cleaners. She shuffles past the florid lounge suites and the rows of Formica-topped kitchen tables, and the slightly chipped, still-unsold porcelain swan, and she doesn't stop until she reaches the slamlock security gate to the office in the corner where Mr. Sher and Mr. Rubin have locked themselves in. There she stands, bent metal tray in her hands, and rattles the gate with her foot.

From behind his desk Harry glances up from punching numbers. "Aaah Beauty, *dumela* Beauty, tea time already," he says, greeting her in her own language, and twirling his keys and striding down the plastic runner to unlock the gate.

He is almost back to his desk when he turns, animated, to face Jack.

"Rubin!" he says.

"Pardon?" says Jack, dragging his cup of tea towards him.

"I've just had a brilliant idea."

"Go on."

"Let's send out a special invitation to all our paid-up customers to come in and have a cup of tea and cake in the shop, with an offer to buy anything their heart desires without having to pay a deposit. . . ."

Jack is nodding, an amused smile playing on the corner of his lips.

"We can offer them a free gift, maybe a set of coffee cups, and a fifty-rand discount for any purchase over five hundred rand. And we can pay for their transport to get here as well." He paces up and down the runner, fine-tuning the message. "We mustn't be afraid to lay it on thick, Rubin, thick, to say what wonderful customers they've been. What do you think, Mr. Pink?"

"Not bad," says Jack, grinning broadly. "I like it. I could have sworn I suggested something similar last week."

Glossary

Yiddish to English

bobbeh-meissehs	*baw-beh mei-sehs*	old wives' tales
ganef	*gah-nef*	thief, crook
ganovim	*gah-novim*	thieves (pl)
chazzisher	*chah-zehr-sher*	junk, piggish, mess
shlemiel	*shli-meel*	inept person
shmaltz	*shmahlts*	animal fat
shmuck	*shmuk*	penis, idiot, self-made fool
shnorrer	*shnaw-rehr*	cheapskate, miser
shtetl	*shteht-l*	small town
shtik	*shtick*	oomph
shtum	*shtoom*	mute, dumb, quiet

Source: Fred Kogos, *A Dictionary of Yiddish Slang & Idioms,* (Secaucus, N.J.: Citadel Press, 1967)

Afrikaans to English

bang	*bung*	scared, afraid
jol	*jawl*	party, have a good time
lekker	*lecker*	nice
pap en vleis	*pup en flayse*	maize-meal and meat
pomp	*pawmp*	have sexual intercourse
smaaked	*smaaked*	liked
the manne	*the munna*	the men (macho)
woes	*voes*	angry
vuil	*fail*	dirty, guilty, dishonest
yusses	*yuss-ess*	term of surprise, of exclamation